180 degrees

degrees

Emerging from
Childhood Darkness

PRAISE FOR
180 DEGREES

"In her memoir, Danielle Saintard Valiente recounts her small but stalwartly self, darting in and out of environments, some fraught with torment, others with precarious security. Her undeniable refusal to succumb to the chaos around her is exactly what gives her the momentum to rise above it. Her autobiography is a must read for teachers and other child advocates who want to gain more insight into children who mask distress. Soft, subtle signs of domestic abuse can make recognizing it difficult. This book helps readers peer beyond the obvious."

Ingrid L. Wiemer, PhD
Retired Teacher, Principal, Executive Director, and University Education Adjunct Instructor

"*180 Degrees* is a powerful memoir that had me riveted to its pages. Danielle's vulnerability, courage, and strength shine brilliantly, as she walks you through her two worlds — one full of darkness, secrets, and unimaginable pain; and the other full of hope, dreams, and wonder. Danielle's life has been an incredible journey of the human spirit, of sacrifice, and of perseverance, and this book will leave you with a faith that all things are possible."

Penny Tate
Mental Health Specialist, Educator, and Co-Author of *Manifesting Your Dreams: Inspiring Words of Encouragement, Strength and Perseverance*

"This book brings enormous hope to those who suffer from trauma. Through the author's narrative, we see the power of believing in inner strength and resilience. When the outer world denies help, there is the inner world to rescue one from traumatic scars by redefining, reshaping, and moving from dark to the light."

Marcia Guimaraes
Licensed Clinical Mental Health Counselor, Certified Redecision Therapist, Advanced Integrative Therapy Practitioner

"From the moment I began reading Danielle Saintard Valiente's memoir, *180 Degrees*, all five of my senses were engaged. Imagining myself in Danielle's place, I was gripped by dread, powerlessness, and a chilling emptiness that no child should ever have to endure. The fact that Danielle was able to overcome a life spent in 'survival mode' to become the brilliant, driven, and empowered woman she is today is a testament to the resilience of the human spirit. Together as readers of this intensely personal and inspiring book, we grieve her lost childhood and celebrate the woman Danielle was determined to become."

Stacey Sassine
Grief Support Specialist and Founder of One Million Monarchs, a Youth Bereavement Organization

"*180 Degrees* is honest, bravely authentic, and heartbreaking -- yet full of hope and healing in its pages. Danielle's book is a must-read for anyone on a journey to better understand or personally overcome the ravages of childhood abuse and neglect."

Crystal Sutherland
Author of *Journey to Heal: Seven Essential Steps of Recovery for Survivors of Childhood Sexual Abuse*

"This book grabbed onto me and would not let go! It's raw, courageous and authentic."

Colonel Rob Campbell, U.S. Army Retired
Leadership Consultant and Author of the Books *It's Personal, Not Personnel*; *At Ease*; and *Left and Right of the Boom*

"In my experience, domestic abuse takes place in adult relationships, with children witnessing the violence and living in fear. Danielle Saintard Valiente casts light on a whole new category of abuse for me. In her life, her whole dysfunctional family — father, mother, brother, grandmother, aunts and uncles — turned on a vulnerable little girl.

Did she seem *Other* to them? Were they frightened that she was different? Was intelligent and creative, drawn to a different kind of life? Did they feel the need to contain or destroy the *Outcast*?

I don't know. Perhaps no one ever will. And this knowledge is bone-chilling.

Victim. Fighter. Survivor. Shape-Shifter. For me, these powerful words describe Danielle —the child, the teen, the young adult. Somehow, she escaped with body and soul intact. *Pluck. Tenacity. Determination. Courage.* These are the qualities that keep her going ... that keep all survivors going. I applaud her willingness to share her story and to help us learn."

Karen A. Szymanski, PhD
President of Gateways Learning, Inc., and Retired Board President and Longtime Volunteer for A Safe Place, a Chicago-Area Domestic Violence Prevention and Response Agency

"*180 Degrees: Emerging Childhood from Darkness* illustrates the very real impact of childhood trauma experiences and of growing up in families that we continually count on, trust, and are disappointed by — time-after-time-after-time. Danielle Saintard Valiente is a 'survivor-to-thriver' — courageous, bold, and caring enough to retell her own stories so that others might heal. Her memoir will inspire you to champion over challenge! Danielle shows us that even what we fear is broken — like a mosaic — is just waiting to for us to assemble into a perfectly imperfect work of art."

Amy L. Feath, VSP
Executive Director, The Carousel Center – A Child Advocacy Center in Wilmington, NC

"Danielle Saintard Valiente is a blessing, a marvel, and a force of nature. The lessons we can learn from her experiences, observations, and character – and then apply to ourselves and the world around us – are profound. Her candid and inspiring account of emerging from childhood darkness will bring you to tears and to laughter, to shock and to hope, to anger and to gratitude. *180 Degrees* is *her* story, but this book is *our* gift. There is nothing quite so powerful as a woman standing up to a cold, indifferent world to say: 'Here I am and I'm no longer afraid.'"

Kate Colbert
Marketing Consultant, Communications Coach, Former Domestic Violence Advocate, and Business Author

180 degrees

Emerging from Childhood Darkness

DANIELLE SAINTARD VALIENTE

Silver Linings MEDIA

180 Degrees: Emerging from Childhood Darkness

By Danielle Saintard Valiente

Copyright 2020 by Danielle Saintard Valiente

Published by Silver Tree Publishing, a division of
Silver Tree Communications, LLC (Kenosha, WI), under its
Silver Linings Media imprint for memoirs.

www.SilverTreePublishing.com

Stories shared in this book are based on actual events and are
recounted to the best of the author's recollection. Some names
and details have been changed.

Editing by:
Kate Colbert

Cover design and typesetting by:
Courtney Hudson

First edition, January 2021

ISBN: 978-1-948238-34-2

Library of Congress Control Number: 2020925468

Created in the United States of America

DEDICATION

To those who have contributed toward the healing of childhood trauma,
I dedicate this book. It is not an easy path, but you chose it selflessly.
I applaud you and thank you for continuing to change so many lives ...
picking up the slack for those who failed our children.

CONTENTS

Part 3

FOREWORD

By Amy L. Feath, VSP

As the Executive Director of The Carousel Center — a child advocacy center that coordinates the investigation, prosecution, and treatment of the most severe cases of child abuse in our Wilmington, North Carolina, region — the most frequent question I hear from non-offending adult caregivers is, "Will she be 'broken' from this for the rest of her life?"

The short answer is a resounding "No." The longer answer — which is explored powerfully in this remarkable book by childhood abuse and neglect survivor Danielle Saintard Valiente — teaches us that it's indeed possible to turn hurt into hope ... that incredible, healthy, joyful, fulfilling lives often follow a very dark past, and that previous victimization does not preclude future strength and peace.

Nearly a decade ago, I accepted the challenge to rally our community in Wilmington, North Carolina, (the town where Danielle landed after college) to build The Carousel Center for kids who have experienced physical and sexual abuse and neglect. Hopeful as always, even I was concerned about how I would be able to see devastated, injured, terrified children each day and stay the course. In the end, devastation and terror are not the hallmarks of what I've experienced at all. The work we do is full of love and hope, happiness and wholeness. I never cease to be amazed by what Carousel's children teach me every day about the ability to love and find forgiveness for those who have done unspeakable damage. Our children possess an unyielding connection to possibility and hope, and they are instinctively and perpetually on a path to find joy in life. We who work with them learn far more from each one of these child survivors — about resilience, courage, and forgiveness — than we could ever teach them.

If this thought gives you hope, then *180 Degrees: Emerging from Childhood Darkness* by Danielle Saintard Valiente will not disappoint. *180 Degrees* illustrates the very real impact of childhood trauma experiences and of growing up in families that continually disappoint us (time after time after time) when we count on them and trust them to care for us. *180 Degrees* exemplifies the resilient spirits our children possess instinctively. What's happened *to* you doesn't limit or *define* you!

Danielle is a true champion for our community's children, choosing Carousel Center as a beneficiary of her time, energies, and talents. She knows that children living in the footsteps of her traumatic childhood need and deserve a safe place, and she has helped us to build that here in her new hometown. She's a "survivor-to-thriver" in countless ways — many of which you will see demonstrated through the stories in this revealing book. I am inspired that Danielle has been courageous, bold, and caring enough to share her own personal journey in the following pages. She serves as a living, breathing example of a child survivor never giving up on her dreams yet struggling with complex (and often conflicting) emotions surrounding her born family.

This book will inspire you to lean into the truth of your experiences and personal scars, to allow yourself to live fully, pursue your dreams, and love. Most of all, I hope Danielle's memoir will inspire you to "champion over challenge!" Because no matter how much or how little trauma you have experienced, you too have struggled and you too can overcome. Danielle shows us that, like a beautiful mosaic, even what we fear is broken is just waiting to for us to assemble into a perfectly imperfect work of art.

It is an honor to know Danielle personally and to call her a friend, and it is a privilege to introduce her and her stories to you, her readers. Danielle is an inspiration to me and many. Let yourself be moved and encouraged by the vulnerable, raw, empowering account that awaits you in *180 Degrees: Emerging from Childhood Darkness*.

Amy L. Feath, VSP
Executive Director, The Carousel Center
Wilmington, North Carolina

PROLOGUE

Long before a heart-stopping Valentine's Day nightmare in the year 2020, I was one of millions of people who already thought Valentines' Day was overrated. Frankly, I'd be okay skipping right over February 14th. But there was no skipping it this year. As I settled into the new year, I realized that, for the first time, I had everything I had worked for and dreamt of. Then suddenly, I was only 10 minutes away from losing it all.

For the first time in my life, I had love, family, safety, security, and a promising future. It took me 32 years to get there. I had just arrived, in every sense of the word.

 For the first time in my life, I had love, family, safety, security, and a promising future. It took me 32 years to get there. I had just arrived, in every sense of the word.

It feels like yesterday when I was sleeping on the floor of my office with my dog, Cooper, with no home to call my own. Still, every time I pull into my driveway, I am in shock that this is mine, and there's no denying that the shock beats the fear of being homeless, hungry, and poor. Finally, I am no longer overwhelmed by negative thoughts swirling around in my subconscious, jumping through the crevasses, and creating these hypothetical visions of catastrophe striking again.

All under one roof, in my dream home in my dream neighborhood, I have my husband, my two rescue pups, our friend Davey, cabinets full of food, and all the evidence of two years of hard work all around me. We live under the trees and by the creek — and I am reminded daily of the woods and creek behind my house as a child. They were my safe place; they were the destination to which I ran when I was scared or in danger. The fact that I now live in a beautiful home on a property with old trees, a pond, and creek — but without the danger, abuse, or neglect atop the hill in the dark home of my childhood — feels like it carries such purpose. *I got my safe place back.*

Davey and I have been friends for around 10 years. We both lived in the same apartment complex in 2010, which was my first apartment when I arrived, fresh out of college, in Wilmington, North Carolina. My dog, Cooper, ran up to Davey and jumped on his lap, and his lap was in a wheelchair. I was nervous that Cooper was going to hurt Davey, but Davey joyfully accepted every Cooper kiss and, after that, we became friends.

Davey's use of a wheelchair goes back to his childhood. He suffered a spinal cord injury in a trampoline accident at the age of 15, which left him paraplegic. As of the writing of this book, he was 37 and one of my closest friends.

When JP and I became serious in our relationship, I told him that I wanted Davey to live with us one day. When he quickly agreed, it confirmed to me that JP's big heart was the one I was meant to fall in love with, but I also knew that one day, we would give Davey a nicer place to live, in his own apartment without roommates, with a big handicap-accessible shower and a family to spend birthdays and holidays with. Davey was a family member that I got to choose, and on May 1, 2019, Davey moved into his new handicap-accessible apartment at our home.

Fast-forward nine months, and it was Friday, February 14, 2020, and a cold front had come through. The air was chilly and dry, around 40 degrees. Our gas torch light was glowing outside our citronella-yellow front door, along with the white lights twinkling through the ivy archway that warmed the entrance to the brick pathway that led to Davey's apartment on the back side of our house.

It started out as a quiet Friday night. After a long day at work, JP and I met in our kitchen at 7:30 p.m. for some pepperoni pizza from our favorite pizza restaurant, Mellow Mushroom, before we headed up to the third floor of the house to watch a movie. I changed into an oversized striped sweater, sweatpants, and tall fuzzy socks — none of which matched. The moonlight was sneaking through the leaves above our roof and into the dormer window at the top of the stairs that landed on the third floor, where the painted wood planks creaked beneath our feet. Our dogs, Cruz and Clarke, were chewing their bones, independently, one on each bean bag.

About an hour into the movie, JP smelled something burning and it seemed to be coming through the vent. We both jolted up from our sunken-in seats to run through each room on the second floor, then the first, hoping that our old 1949 brick colonial was not experiencing an electrical fire. I was terrified.

We followed the smell to the kitchen, where the singed and smoky odor was flowing from the vent on the wall shared between our house and Davey's apartment. It smelled like *really* burnt popcorn. JP looked out our sliding door on the back side of our house, where he could easily see 12 feet down into Davey's glass door, and he saw the back of Davey's home healthcare worker. She was sitting on the loveseat. We both breathed a sigh of relief, assuming they had burned popcorn and that everything was okay. Davey was not alone. But we returned to the third floor to check our phones just in case Davey had needed us. And he had. A three-way text from Davey was only the beginning of the Valentine's Day nightmare.

"Hey, are you guys home? My worker isn't answering me, and she left hotdogs burning on the stove."

I hurtled down both flights of stairs, with my feet barely touching the treads. I flew out the front door in my socks and, as I was about to go under the arch around the corner, I stopped abruptly. There was someone in the healthcare worker's car. The seat was fully reclined, so I banged on the window, screaming, "WAKE UP, HE'S IN THERE!" over and over. To my surprise, a man who I had never seen before was sleeping in the worker's driver's seat, in my driveway, at 9:00 p.m. on Valentine's Day. With one eye open, he sleepily murmured the words, "*Who* is in there?"

UH OH.

As I crossed under the arch, I heard the smoke alarm in Davey's apartment sounding with its telltale screech. Behind our house is a flower bed, edged with a dense perimeter of monkey grass, which follows the brick pathway around the houseline and lands at Davey's door. I ran around the bend, panicked. *Who is he? Where is she? Davey!!!*

The smoke was so thick that I could not see the walls of the apartment. I opened the sliding door, holding my breath, seeing the worker sound asleep on the loveseat to the right of the door, with her head on a pile of clothes, and her snore echoing almost louder than the smoke detector. I did not see Davey, so in that second of panic, I thought I was going to find him dead, under my own roof, while I was home. I couldn't breathe.

I ran to the bathroom, finding Davey on the toilet, where the healthcare worker had left him for his routine session of privacy. He was on the phone with 911, coughing and unable to talk because the bathroom door was open and the black smoke was traveling straight from the stovetop into his lungs. He was unable to escape and get to safety. He had been there for hours.

My sense of panic sent a throbbing sensation through my chest and veins. I do not work well under pressure and I did not know how to get Davey's chair unhooked from the toilet. This is why he had certified nursing assistants (CNAs) in the first place. I needed help, so I grabbed his phone and ran. On my way out of the apartment, the mystery man from the drive- way had come inside and he was shaking the sleeping worker, screaming her name, saying, "What is wrong with you?? WAKE UP! WAKE UP!"

As I was on the phone with 911, having taken over the call from Davey, I ran into a herd of firefighters on the brick pathway, so I turned around to show them where Davey was. By this time, the smoke had started to clear out of the apartment through the door I had left wide open. The firemen were able to get Davey's chair detached from the toilet, and they wheeled him outside, where I watched them attach an apparatus to his mouth, full of tubes, as they worked furiously to clear the smoke from his lungs. Davey sat there unclothed in his wheelchair, in the 40-degree weather, in front of 12 firemen, two officers, his negligent worker, the mystery man, JP, and me. I grabbed blankets and a sweatshirt from the house, and the mystery man was helping me cover him. Meanwhile, the worker was on the phone with her supervisor and the apartment was being ventilated with giant fans hooked up to the windows.

I held onto Davey's shoulders, then collapsed onto the ground. My vision blurred, as I started to hyperventilate and cry uncontrollably. It was another anxiety attack. It had been years since my last. I started screaming, "I thought you were dead, I thought you were dead!" A firefighter grabbed a chair and had me sit, while I buried my face in my hands, muting the decibels of my scream.

"Ma'am, are there dogs in the house? Your house is filling with smoke and I think I saw a puppy run up the stairs and I can't find her."

OH MY GOD. The second round of rescuing the helpless — now my canine CHILDREN!

Cruz was two years old and we had rescued him the previous year, but Clarke, Cruz's newly adopted sister, we had just rescued three weeks prior. She weighed about five pounds.

I ran back inside the front door that was left open. The firefighters were racing around, opening all the windows. Cruz ran straight into my arms; I clutched him to my chest and screamed "CLARKE!!! CLARKE!!!"

Her little black paws tiptoed down the stairs. She was shaking, but happy to see her mom, so I grabbed her too, which left with me carrying 35 pounds in my arms, jogging to the back of the house in my socks. I felt nothing but relief. I would put myself through a blazing fire to save my dogs. I love them that much.

JP was speaking to the police officer, and as she finished taking down his name and phone number, she requested mine, telling me that she had called DSS (i.e., the Department of Social Services), where she filed a case of neglect against the healthcare worker.

The firemen completed Davey's health check and as they started making their way back to their trucks, one of them pulled me aside.

"I want to show you something. Can you please come inside with me for a minute?"

I followed him inside the apartment.

"Look at this pot. There is no water left in here and this charred bottom does not even resemble hotdogs. She must have been asleep for at least 45 minutes. Then, look at this. There is this pot full of grease, only one burner away. With the way that smoke was coming off that burner, in about 10 minutes, this pot of grease would have caught on fire and this entire house could have burnt down."

TEN MINUTES.

My life, as you are about to learn, had been a series of traumas — of catastrophes and loss, abuse and neglect, moments of rock bottom, and so many times when I couldn't breathe. And just as I was beginning to enjoy the safety and stability of a life that was 180 degrees from what I'd endured as a child, Davey's home health worker took us 10 minutes from the unthinkable. She nearly took everything away from me — my friend, my husband, my home, my pets, and perhaps my own life too. In truth, I'm not sure we would have made it down from the third floor if the structure was fully engulfed by the time we knew something was wrong. It had taken me 32 years to create this life, and I was only 10 minutes away from losing it all. This was my biggest trigger yet, because it forced me to face everything from the past 32 years. There was so much to process, so I started writing this book.

Part 1
ZERO DEGREES

Even when fully bathed in light, some of us can still sense the darkness — heavy, eerie, daunting, inevitable. Victims of the universe, we know that night always falls.

But when darkness comes, even the smallest glimmer of light can save us ... warm, hopeful, a reminder of who we are and what is possible. The light may dim, but not easily or without a fight. So we keep fighting.

As we move from darkness to light — emerging to new possibilities while healing and overcoming — we may someday find ourselves aglow with peace and brightness that can no longer succumb to the dark. We shine as if we have never seen the other side. And the longer our light shines without being dimmed, the stronger it grows. We can — and do — overcome. We eclipse our past.

Middle-Class

Growing up in the "middle class," where
   the paychecks
went to cigarettes and beer,
I lived two lives.
The food was cheap and easy,
McDonald's 20-pieces, Hostess Ho Hos,
   Oreos, and Pepsi two-liters.
When Dad was at work, the lady who
   gave birth to me
bought a swimming pool. Two
   weeks later,
the pool was green — "no money for
   that chlorine ..."

The house was big and the yard was
   bigger,
but the inside was never clean. Junk
   piled up
and the kids raised themselves while
   I developed OCD.
Sister went barefoot on the motorized
   scooter
and paid for delivery pizza with
   a double handful of pennies.
Brother and I had a paper route in the
   projects at 11 and 12
because the lady said she couldn't pay
   the bills.
She always had her garden flowers and
   cigarettes though,
while everything else was put on
   layaway:
        the Kmart clothes, the little
        Christmases, and
        the furniture.

This middle class, it went away so fast
when we bought the house on
   Birchcroft Road.
The cars blew up and the winters
   were rough,
and the doors were always closed.
Don't open windows! Don't use the heat!
   Don't even come through the door!
I never came home,
I bought my own clothes.
My friends gave me dinner, rides, and
   holidays.
The house showed well, the garden
   was full,
but the pool was green and the house
   was not clean
and the cars wouldn't start.

No water, no fruit, no vegetables,
no shampoo on the shelves.
Fend for yourselves!
This included the dog,
who stayed tied to a tree.
Like me, he probably just wanted to be
   set free.

I always wanted to be in the
   middle class,
but not the kind my parents crafted.
That middle class, it went so fast,
and ended in bankruptcy.
My soul saw light through the windows
(because I opened them when no one
   was home).
I snuck out at night and came home to
   fights,
And I knew this was poverty.

Dark Holes

I knew I was different from them — the family I was born into. My father was an abusive alcoholic who died of ALS when I was 16. My "mother" was 11 years younger than he, becoming a widow at 41. She had what we believed to be multiple personality disorder and untreated post-partum. My brother is a sociopathic addict. And my sister is a compulsive liar who lives in the victim world, so desperate to create her own "normal" life yet so unwilling to take accountability for her own behaviors. Then there is me — I am the oldest child in this family, with the exception of my half-brother, who was my dad's son from a one-night stand. He was only part of our lives here and there, and we never considered each other siblings.

My family didn't like how I was different from them. In the house, I was the bad kid, while in school I was the good student. I was branded the black sheep by the age of 12 and lived in between the lines of OCD, radiating anger, and severe anxiety for the first 18 years of my life. For as long as I can remember, I had big dreams of making it into the hands of a foster family. When my first dream didn't come true, I raised my standards — along with my self-esteem — and followed the tunnel of optimism, my first step in getting the hell out of there. I had my college dreams come true, then moved 800 miles down the east coast where I hid from everyone and everything I knew. I used my work ethic, the most important thing I learned in Massachusetts, and began climbing the ladder of entrepreneurship during my last few weeks of being 25. I beat a lawsuit at the age of 26, became homeless many times, and by the age of 31, I was married, living in the home of my dreams, and had built a million-dollar company. It had been a life of extremes. Of the darkest darkness and the brightest redeeming light.

How Did I Get Here?

I was conditioned to find a way out of dark holes. But there was no dark hole as dark or as vast as the place I grew up.

 I was conditioned to find a way out of dark holes. But there was no dark hole as dark or as vast as the place I grew up.

Let's go back.

I grew up in a suburb an hour outside of Boston, Massachusetts. Leominster was the home to Johnny Appleseed, the leading manufacturer of the plastic comb and where the pink flamingo lawn ornament was invented. It was far from being an exciting environment. We didn't have the beach or the mountains, but we did have the three Ms: mall, movies, and McDonald's. The best part of being in the suburbs was that we had land and trees. I loved the woods behind my house, with hilltops of pine and birch, with the creek in the valley below. We had many safe neighborhoods, which were bustling with children riding bikes, rollerblading, and running through the summer streets barefoot. It was a time when we could leave our bikes in the front yard overnight; we could walk for hours to the donut shop and we would waste our summer days waiting for the most reliable adult we knew — the ice cream man.

Side-yard after-school flag football and summer-night flashlight tag games were the most exciting of times. I was often the only girl, but I was okay with that because I learned how to throw a decent spiral. Skin cancer was not a popular topic yet, so we lathered up in baby oil and baked on the pavement to sizzle along with summer. You could cook an egg on that pavement, so you had to get your summer feet ready at the right time, so you didn't get third-degree burn. (Where I come from, it's a rite of passage to prep your "summer feet," building up callouses so you could walk on the hot pavement.)

Fall gave us so many opportunities, like raking. Yes, raking. When you can rake the entire yard into one large pile beside a trampoline, there is no better motivation for yardwork. We would jump for hours, playing popcorn, and showing off every kind of flip we could invent.

In the winter, the igloos and snowball fights kept us warm. I swear, as kids we never felt temperature. We would, however, shiver by the bus stop, but only because school was not canceled unless it was -10 degrees.

The spring always came late, mostly washed away by too much rain and lost blooms. The groundhog always kept us eager with all fingers crossed, year after year, but he never seemed to repair our broken optimism. New England winters were always long and brutal.

For me, there was never a care in the world … outside the house. I tried to stay outside as many hours as possible, because once I walked through the darkness of the front door, it was like the universe shifted and I shifted right along with it. I lived in two completely different worlds and I felt like I was living two different lives … with two different versions of Danielle. I promise to introduce you to them both.

Who Was in the Hole

The Lady:

(Short for "the lady who gave birth to me," because that is all she ever was.)

A wrinkled face with thick, frizzy salt-and-pepper hair, green eyes, and freckled skin. Shy, solemn, and troubled. A state prison correctional officer. Petite. Green thumb, sewer, smoker. A never completer — many things started, but never finished. A reader and TV watcher. A sitter. A hider. A liar. An emotional and physical abuser. Disconnected from herself, her family, and the world. Fragile. Broken, with no one to repair her. Loveless.

Dad:

A baby face, light hair turned gray early, blue eyes and a muscular build. An athlete, a construction worker, a rock music lover. (Oh yeah, Pearl Jam.) A worker. A laugh snorter, pool player, and mower of lawns. An alcoholic, a smoker, an addict of all things hereditary. Abuser on drunk nights, and angry during sober mornings. Scary and enjoyable, depending on how many Miller Lites he'd already had. Didn't know how to love, but wanted to. ALS victim. 1953-2005.

Brother:

A brown-haired, brown-eyed Irish twin of mine. Athlete of all sports. Video game player, junk food junkie, movie line reciter. Fast runner, physically strong, and naturally talented at just about everything. Sports first, school second. Follower, pleaser, addict, abuser. My best friend and my worst enemy. Angry, violent, Jekyll and Hyde, Bonnie and Clyde (with The Lady). Adrenaline seeker in all activities, including abuse. Love seeker in all the wrong places and/or things.

Sister:

Blonde, blue-eyed, and baby faced. Seven years younger than me. Cute, tiny, Tinkerbell meets tomboy. Attention seeker — both positive and negative. The "mistake," according to our parents. Spontaneous, fearless, hopeless romantic. Crowd pleaser and follower. Chameleon. School skipper, rebel without a cause. Living day by day. Liar, manipulator, victim. Desperate for love, attention, and the idea of a perfect life.

Me:

Back then, I was a brown-haired, brown-eyed, petite girl with freckled cheeks. Gosh, I hated my freckles, my small eyes, my big nose, and my flat chest. Stubborn. Very stubborn. A full-time socialite and part-time nerd. Straight-A student, member of the gifted and talented and future problem solver's club, science fair winner. Eye roller, attitude always on standby. A leader, bossy, but scrappy. Always smiling and always active. A dancer, a singer, and an over achiever. A believer in perfection. Emotions were creepy. Secretary of student government — a planner, organizer, and a fundraising princess. A budding tennis player, a sport's game cheerleader (unofficial, of course). A worker. Always a worker. Responsible, determined, and restless. (Rest was for the dead, so they say.) Impatient, grudge-holder for unfairness, corruption, or disloyalty — fairness-seeker Libra. A good friend, a loyal friend, and a thoughtful friend. People lover with a maternal instinct.

In costume for my very first dance recital at Heidi Hogan's Dance Studio

The Atmosphere

"You should go kill yourself."

Good thing I was so stubborn.

She persisted, "You're a cold-hearted bitch. You're going to go to hell," said the lady who gave birth to me.

I have a hard time saying the words mom and mother. It's a title that needs to be earned.

There was always this alliance with The Lady and my brother. They were like Bonnie and Clyde after my dad passed. My brother was my dad's favorite *and* The Lady's favorite. I guess because he was the only boy, the middle child, not a mistake and not me. When our dad got sick, my brother told us he had to take his place, which wasn't a good place to take. He carried on the abuse, started smoking the same cigarettes, and drinking the same beer. Our dad was not a role model, but that was all my brother knew. There was no one in our circle for us to look up to.

There was no one in our circle for us to look up to.

My brother took Dad's illness the hardest. He was arrested often. He was dealing drugs at age 12 and couldn't seem to keep himself out of trouble. By high school, he was an addict. Alcohol and marijuana were certainly his gateway drugs. After I went to college, he wanted nothing to do with me. My sister said he would still bring up how unfair it was that I had the biggest bedroom. He was angry, over everything, and his coping mechanism was drugs and alcohol. From what I heard and read in the newspapers, my brother has been on every drug under the sun, he has been linked to prostitutes, he dated a woman 30 years his senior with five children (who were once living in my childhood basement), lived in a tent in our backyard, sold his roommate's car for drug money and then has the obvious expected arrests, restraining orders, and an unhealthy relationship with a girlfriend, leading to a custody battle over the daughter they shared. The list goes on, but he was truly just a product of his upbringing. We all were.

So why was I so bad?

Well, I had an attitude. If I was yelled at, I yelled back. If I was screamed at, I screamed back, *even louder*. If I was told to go kill myself, I repeated the same threat back. I was trying to stand up for myself, but I just fell in the trap of adapting to my surroundings. I am not proud of this. This is the reason why it took me 15 years to understand that I was conditioned to be a product of my environment, just like my siblings.

I was a child and I hated who I was. In my house, I was a bad person. I was angry, loud, and spiteful. Outside of my house, I was free and safe to be myself, to be a kid. I was quiet, kind, and sweet. I was constantly switching between

The house I grew up in, 99 Birchcroft Road, my bedroom in the top right corner

both Danielles, but when I was outside of the house, thinking about who I was inside of the house, I would picture myself yelling and saying horrible things, which made me see myself as extremely ugly. I felt so ugly that I was beyond ashamed; to suppress my shame, I kept everything inside the house a secret.

It wasn't until I was an older teenager that I realized I was living a different life from most. I never told my friends, teachers, or extended family what was happening in the house, mainly because I didn't realize I should have. I only felt comfortable telling the police. It is possible that pride played into this, and I felt like the only ones who could help or keep our little secret were the police.

Over the years, I lost many friends because they didn't understand why I hated my family. This was wrong in their eyes. They had strong relationships with their parents, so how could I possibly hate the lady who gave birth to me when their mom was their best friend? It was hard for them to understand. In their minds, I must have been ungrateful or troubled. There was little to be grateful for.

I knew that once I left for college, I would be safe and it wouldn't matter who knew or who believed me. And then it started happening to my sister. Since I was no longer there to be the object of their ire, Bonnie and Clyde took aim at my little sister. After my sister told me that she was having suicidal thoughts after The Lady had told her to kill herself so many times, I built up the courage to tell my grandmother, but without further investigation, she insisted that this wasn't true. It just couldn't be true. Then came word (possibly rumor, possibly true) that my sister had taken a bottle of Tylenol. She told me that she was having visions of herself hanging from the tree platform that our brother built as a jump spot over the trampoline. She had a piece of paper taped to her chest reading, "*I am so sorry, Danielle.*"

Perfect, Pretty, and Smart

The Lady looked at me and said, "I know why you hate your dad. Because he's not perfect like all your friends. *We* aren't perfect like your friends. You only have perfect, pretty, and smart friends. That is all you care about and you can't accept that your father is in a wheelchair!"

Well, my friends *were* pretty and smart, but they were also 16 years old. For the most part, my friends were in my honors classes, dance classes, and chorus with me. They were the good kids. Unlike my siblings, I was lucky enough to be in a good crowd. The good crowd had good families who took me in for holiday meals, and I relied on them to feed me. They also allowed me to have continual sleepovers and gave me rides so that I was able to leave my house. I was incredibly lucky.

My dad had always been my favorite parent, until I discovered the truth. Shortly after that, he got sick. Before that, my dad seemed to love me when he was moderately sober. He did go with me to the father-daughter dances until middle school and he would tuck me in at night when I was scared of the dark. He would get me home in time to watch *Saved by the Bell* and *Goosebumps* — a major priority. There was a year that my half-brother lived with us and, one time, I told on him for stealing the money out of my piggy bank and that didn't end so well — I saw the two of them fist fighting in our front yard. Another time I sang in a holiday concert and when we got home, my dad told me that he couldn't believe that was *his* daughter on stage ... and that was the only time I ever saw tears in his eyes.

My friend Liesl and I would write songs and perform for him in front of the pool table, while he sat in his recliner holding his trusted can of Miller Lite. He always listened though. Although he didn't hug me, kiss me, or say "I love you," I felt that my dad loved me. He just didn't know how to show love. He was too busy covering up his own emotions and pain from his past, where his alcoholic father abused him and passed on his demons, not to just one generation but two.

I remember it clearly when I heard the word "alcoholic." I was sitting in 5th grade guidance class, and I truly did not know what that was. The guidance counselor was reading a story about alcoholism and she was reading a passage about the behaviors of an alcoholic and a child's bodily response to addiction. The words began to sound fuzzy and I felt everything go numb. I mentally blacked out. The light bulb went off — *holy shit, my dad is an alcoholic!!!*

I ran home from the bus, barging through the front door and running into the living room where The Lady slept on a sofa every day for as long as I had remembered.

"Dad is an alcoholic!!! HELLO!!! Dad is an alcoholic!!!"

There was no response, but I successfully woke her, which was a miracle. The Lady could sleep through multiple fire alarms, and when we were little and the school nursed called home, no one ever answered (which meant I spent sick days sleeping in the nurse's office instead of at home in my own bed).

"DID YOU KNOW that *DAD* is an alcoholic???"

She stared in complete shock and silence. I had my answer. Like all the dysfunctions in my family, we just weren't going to talk about it.

Eventually, my dad lost his voice and I wish I could say it was from all the yelling. I believe I was 11 and we were in the McDonald's drive-through when I realized something was wrong. My dad was trying to order, but his voice kept cracking and then nothing would come out. He kept trying, but no words followed. I yelled at him, "Dad, order the food! You're holding up the line!" Months later, he was diagnosed with ALS (amyotrophic lateral sclerosis), also known as Lou Gehrig's disease. It was a battle he would fight for almost six years.

Cold-Hearted

The Lady reiterated that I would regret not talking to him before he died. I told her that was not true because I had lost my dad a long time ago, to alcohol. I told her she didn't know anything, like how he would hit us at night when he was drunk, after she had left to work the night shift.

"You're a cold-hearted bitch." Those are the words I most remember from that conversation. I thought, but didn't say, *"It takes one to know one."*

"You're a cold-hearted bitch." Those are the words I most remember from that conversation. I thought, but didn't say, "It takes one to know one."

The Lady worked the night shift at a women's prison an hour from our house. She would typically leave before 9:30 p.m. and spend her night and early morning watching prison cells, a warden of the incarcerated peace. Sometimes she would leave me at the kitchen table with Shake 'n Bake pork chops and tell me I "will SLEEP at the table" if I did not eat everything on my plate. I was stubborn and my tastebuds were too. Once she left, I would feed the dog under the table and sneak upstairs.

By this time of night, there were 30 cans of Miller Lite in the trash, including the cardboard box at the top, which meant Dad had drunk the last can. He would get angry — invariably about something that had nothing to do with us — and my brother and I would meet the leather belt for more frequent flyer miles or end up in the kitchen for something worse. I watched as my brother was thrown — fast and aggressively — against the kitchen wall, like he was a towel swatting and killing a fly. Other times, our dad would make us kneel on the kitchen floor, with our feet held up, as our knees ached and bruised. We had to be perfectly silent. Sometimes it would be hours until he went to bed, while other times we only waited and suffered until he passed out in the recliner, with a cigarette falling out of his hand.

As it got closer to my dad's passing, The Lady called me while I was at my cousin Kim's house and told me that I *had* to speak with my dad because I was the reason he was staying alive and suffering.

"Danielle, *you* are the reason he is dying."

At this point, my dad was in a hospice facility, without the ability to speak. The Lady wanted me to talk to him, as a one-sided conversation, to *allow* my dad to die. I didn't feel it was my responsibility to give anyone permission to die — wasn't that their choice? Or a matter of fate? When he was ready, he would pass.

I watched this slow process that ALS unfurls for its victims — from losing his voice to the constant falls, to being fired from his job, to getting staples in his head while trying to mop the floor after he became truly disabled, more falls and ambulance rescues. Eventually, he was no longer able to get up the stairs; then he was in a wheelchair with a word chart. In the later stages, our house was turned into a hospital with random people always around, then my dad was taken to hospice after his body and his mind had completely failed him. Now, he was a vegetable. It looked like he had aged 40 years during the past 6.

After that call from The Lady, imploring me to speak with my father, my grandmother called me.

"Danielle, you are going to regret this. You need to talk to your father because once he passes, you will have to live with this regret. Go talk to him."

I caved. Kim's older sister, Tania, drove me to my dad's hospice facility. I wrote him a letter before arriving there and I gave it to his aide, asking her to read it to him once I was gone. I looked at my father, staring into his sad and lonely eyes as he stared back with no voice, no teeth, and white hair. His once-athletic body melted to his wheelchair, like a rotten vegetable caving into itself. His face showed sorrow and an implied, nonverbal apology. Or that's at least what I wanted to imagine. I needed that apology, and we were running out of time.

In the letter, I wrote that I felt he was the reason that I now had lost my brother too, to addiction. I told him that I lost out on my childhood having to be an adult, raising my sister with no concept of what a real family was. I also wrote that I had lost him many years ago and that I had to grow up without either parent truly present. No one to care for me when I was just a child myself.

I remember the last line clearly: *I will never forget, Dad, but I do forgive you. I forgive you.*

A few months later, I received a dozen multi-colored roses on my 16th birthday. They were from my dad. He was still alive, against all odds, and I knew that the workers at his hospice facility had sent the roses. I highly doubt that he used his word chart to request this; the flowers were only the second gift he had ever gotten for me. The first gift had been a set of Spanish CDs. When I was in junior high, I begged my dad to choose a gift for me for Christmas. But, truthfully, he didn't know much about me — other than the fact that I was required to take Spanish in 8th grade. I was disappointed by the CDs because I hated Spanish, but I never showed anything but excitement, because I really wanted him to buy me *more* gifts in the future. And here we were now, with him still in hospice, hanging on much longer than what was predicted, which was possibly a shock to him as well. ALS is a cruel disease and can have a long goodbye.

Even though I didn't want to go to my dad at the hospice facility, I am grateful that my grandmother and The Lady all but obligated me to get into my cousin Tania's car that day. The trip forced me to write that important letter to my dad and to process my emotions and communicate my truth. I felt the forgiveness sinking in, providing both of us some measure of closure. He was coming to terms with ending his 52 years of life and I was gaining emotional freedom, feeling much lighter, as I was now able to start climbing out of the all-encompassing dark hole. This was my first step.

 I felt the forgiveness sinking in, providing both of us some measure of closure.

Safe Place

When I look at the water, it takes me back
to my happy place,
my safe place —
where the light was shining,
the warm glow was grabbing me,
and I knew I was better alone.
A wooden stump sat atop the hill,
the creek at the basin.
The open space,
with trees and no faces.
Where my running feet could rest,
and ground with the earth.
Angelic and beautiful.
The trees
and the running water,
the silence and the fresh air —
They will never know
the gifts they gave me.

② Thumper

I would run through the backyard grass — behind the dog (chained between two trees), past the dirt that dipped before it sloped, through the birches, and to the cleared landing in the woods. The sun would shine through like angels were surrounding me, with the tree stump at the top of the hill and a panoramic view of the creek that meandered and followed,

My safe place, the woods

through the pines and banks of rich soil. I would run over the double-log bridges, always on the hunt for branches adequate for my tree forts, which were built on the dirt, but designed well and swept daily. (Yes, I swept the dirt.) That grass, that hill, those trees — I ran through them sometimes with joy, but often with terror, looking over my shoulder. Games of chase or "tag" during my childhood were rarely games at all. They were acts of survival.

As I write this book, it has been 15 years since my feet felt that terrain, but I can still feel that dip and slope leading to the hill that overlooked a sort of nothingness — the feeling of world peace and a moment to catch my breath. My eyes can still see the purity in the white birch bark against the summer's green leaves. My skin can still feel the encompassing warm glow that instantly made me feel safe, even if just for a moment.

I would run so fast, not looking back, until I made it to the tree stump. There was only one problem — *he was always faster than me.*

Just before my feet could leave the grass, he grabbed my shirt and pulled me back with aggressive force. He was the embodiment of evil, with black beady eyes and a yell that would set me on silent. I began to quiver as he spat in my face, waiting for a reaction, but I froze. I began to black out when he started jumping on my stomach, like a trampoline, until I threw up. Then, he spat again and walked away.

That was the first time.

His anger fueled his adrenaline. The adrenaline fed his veins with power and there was no possible way for me to escape. He knew that if I yelled, The Lady would probably sleep through it and he wouldn't be caught. But just in case, he would cover my mouth with his foot.

When *Buffy the Vampire Slayer* debuted on TV, my newest idol was an ass-kicking Sarah Michelle Gellar. I hoped that I could be strong like her. I would watch the new episodes every Tuesday night, simultaneously on the phone with friends discussing each scene, because it could not wait until the morning. Long before social media invented the "watch party," my friends and I were setting trends and reacting in real time. Wednesdays, after school, I would rush to the side yard, where someone had once placed bamboo garden sticks against the house and I couldn't resist. I kicked, snapped, and used the bamboo as pretend daggers for fighting off the vampires, with faces of my brother and the lady who gave birth to me. I would spin, kick, jab, undercut, and aim. I felt more confident now because I had the moves down — choreographed like a bad-ass dance. While I play-acted, I looked just like Buffy, slaying her vamps. When they came for me next time, I was going to be ready.

 When they came for me next time, I was going to be ready.

Clear and Present Danger

My brother vacillated between being my ally and my enemy — tick, tock, tick, tock ... he was Dr. Jekyll then Mr. Hyde. When he was Jekyll, he would invite me to play Wiffle ball, let me sleep on his bedroom floor when I was scared at night, stand up for me against The Lady, and even offer to cook for me and my friends. He and I made pancakes so many nights together for dinner. We were pros — flippin' and sizzlin' like a '50s diner without the milkshakes. And when we wanted lunch food, he was the grill master. When we were younger, I was afraid to use the grill, so he would handle the hotdogs and make them just how I liked them — almost burnt, with slits across the middle, a toasted bun, and extra, extra ketchup. He was just a year younger than me, and people sometimes mistook us for twins.

When he was Hyde, my whole sense of life came crashing down to this simple thought: *Is he going to kill me?* He was only a few inches taller than me. He had a petite frame for a guy, but he was lean and muscular with this secret strength that I never could quite understand. I was hoping to be 5 feet those days, while he was maybe 5'3" and could not have weighed much more than me, especially with these dancer thighs. His thick brown hair was almost never cut, overgrowing his small, intense eyes and coming past the bridge of his large nose, a facial feature he inherited from The Lady (I called it her witch nose). I had freckles and he did not. We both had distinctive cheeks. He had larger lips and less perfect teeth. I seemed to share genetics from both parents, with The Lady's complexion, while his genetics favored The Lady's and my little sister resembled our dad.

When my brother flipped the switch (*tick-tock*) from his doting-brother mode to his abuser persona, he thrived off watching me squirm in fear. If I screamed for help, he smirked. If I tried to hit him, he grabbed my arm, twisted it behind my back, and gave a deep, loud laugh. He dared me to cry. **I never cried.** There was always blacking out.

He knew I would never beat him in a race, so when he wanted to prove his control over me, he would make me race him down the side yard 20 times in a row. Each sprint was a failure for me. I was humbled more by him than anyone. Foot races with my brother were not game-play ... they were a sadistic form of control. If I didn't participate, I would be punished. If I got faster, I would be punished. When I first started getting faster, he sat me on the swing set and told me that he was better than me at everything, and that soon he was going to learn to sing and dance so that he could beat me at that too.

He fit the bill for child-sociopath-gone-adult-serial-killer. Even as a teen, I understood this. I worried this was his destiny and I feared for all his girl-friends —or for anyone who triggered him, really.

One spring day, I was sitting on the rock wall that followed the curve of our steep driveway, a small retention wall that alleviated the height difference of the grass and pavement. Our driveway was a steep hill that dipped down to a basketball hoop on the right and sat up against the garage doors on the left.

My brother had collected toads after it rained and sat me down for what he described as a show. He pulled out handfuls of toads, and before I could say "eww," he began juggling them like a possessed circus clown, celebrating their pre-death encounter. As I started to yell, he grew more excited, throwing each toad, one at a time, as high as he could (which was fright-fully high, considering he had the arm of a pitcher and a quarterback). The toads would fly above two stories, then come crashing down onto the paved driveway, splattering their organs, instantly dead at the scene. I ran away screaming, begging him to stop, but the more I begged, the more toads went flying in the air.

Escape Plan

If I sensed Hyde coming that day, I would sit inside at the computer, using dial-up AOL internet and AIM instant messenger, hiding from this crazy family. My brother waited for that reaction, using the toads to practice his throw and to fulfill his craving of harming something and someone through violence. I sat, listening to the long-awaited sequence of beeping, buzzing, and humming as the modem sprang to life, while toads flew past my face behind the window, showing themselves for a brief second. One thump after another ... another one dead, then another.

I had big dreams of getting out of that house, but sometimes I worried that I would not make it out alive. It shouldn't be this hard. I wondered if the police would ever actually get me out of there. I hoped I would be fostered, adopted, or a successful runaway, but the harsh seasons kept on passing.

In the fall, I made it to the tree stump. Necessity had taught me to run with increased speed. I looked down and saw the thick layer of leaves covering the ground all the way until the creek flowed through, now with colder and clearer water. The water rushed between the rocks as I pictured myself swerving out of his power, like a football play — right, then left, then a fake right, then sprint for a touchdown!

As I was looking at the downhill view, he snuck up behind me. Before I knew it, he was pulling me backward by my shirt, hurling me down the hill, with leaves entering my mouth as I screamed. He chased me down to make sure I kept rolling. My arms were bruising as I tried desperately to keep them tucked around my torso. I was afraid to move a finger out of place. My knees were hitting the uneven ground, and my white sneakers would never look the same. My mind slowed down time and my mouth was rendered mute. With him overhead, laughing, it was like I knew no one could hear me, not even the trees. His power silenced me.

He leaped and forcefully landed on my stomach, jumping until he was satisfied with watching me suffer and left suddenly, after I threw up ... once again.

My brother was a thumper.

Inside the house, there were no hills, but there were stairs. Thirteen, to be exact. I could count them so fast inside my head because I knew he was always only one stair behind. I only had one second to get into the bathroom at the top of the stairs, slam the door, and lock it.

It was the same pattern every time — run, count to 13, enter the bathroom, slam the door as fast as possible with one finger already pressing the lock, plant my feet, lean on the door to hold it shut, silent words "please, please, please." Sometimes, my strength was capable of winning, because I was fed by adrenaline, cortisol, and an overdose of fight-or-flight instinct.

When I did not make it to the bathroom in time, I usually ended up at the bottom of the staircase. The first time he pushed me down, I remember being awake for the first few stairs. I felt my body thumping down — bang,

bang, bang — and my neck felt like it was loosening and separating from the rest of my body. The simple, concussive rhythm put me to sleep, like the thumping of car tires on a back road. The fainting was gentle, like I was being put under with anesthesia and counting backward, but only making it to number 7. I woke up seconds or minutes later, my body crumpled on the carpet by the shoes. He left me there, and no one was home.

The second time it happened, I knew he liked it. His confidence grew because, this time, The Lady was home, but he was not concerned about getting caught. He knew she wouldn't punish him anyway. He threw me down, of course even harder this time, and when I landed, everything went pitch black again. The Lady heard the thumping, woke me up, and sat me in a kitchen chair as my neck dangled and my eyes continued to close.

"Oh, shit. She has a concussion. We need to keep her awake."

I was nauseated and sleepy and kept blowing my nose into a tissue filled with blood and what seemed to be chunks of cartilage. I was fighting it, but my eyes would not stay open. I was so scared. *Please, please, please.*

Counting

My brother and I got in another bad fight.

Per usual, it wasn't about anything important, but when he got angry, it got scary, FAST. I was stuck in the second-floor bathroom with no escape and I heard him running to grab the screwdriver, which he would use to pick the lock. This was his newest discovery —that a locked door was only a temporary problem. I could hear the seconds loudly ticking away in my head. I was always counting.

On this particular day, he was very angry that I locked him out. This was the other battle; he was *already* angry, so if I made it behind the locked door, he would only be angrier once he got to me.

BOOM! He barged through the door, but this time, he had a knife. It was a steak knife from the kitchen. My heartbeat rebounded through my lungs, first through my head, then my feet before it grew a faster-paced rhythm: *thump, thump, thump.*

This was his newest discovery —that a locked door was only a temporary problem. I could hear the seconds loudly ticking away in my head. I was always counting.

This time, he was going to kill me.

My brother led me toward the window in between the tub and the toilet and told me he was either going to stab me or throw me out the window. He popped out the screen and pushed me up against the wall beneath the sill. I had one second to gain protection and add distraction. I managed to grab a hairbrush and I hit him in the head so I could run away.

I ran to my bedroom, because I knew what would have happened if I had attempted the stairs. Before I made it through my door, he pulled me back into the hallway. He was about stab me, so I pushed his head back and it slammed into the floor-length mirror beside us. This bought me enough time to run down the stairs and get outside, where I hurried down the street and into the woods by the street curved, where the tangled vines gave us our own rope swing. My safe spot was no longer a secret, so I stayed in a new spot — hiding behind rocks for what felt like hours, until the thumping stopped. I could stop counting now.

I returned home later that afternoon, when I was sure The Lady would be home and I wouldn't be alone with my brother. Bravely, I told her what happened, hoping that she would make some attempt to keep me safe from her dangerous son. But he had gotten to her first and all she had heard was that I broke a mirror. She furiously told me to pack my stuff — I would be moving in with my Uncle Greg and my new Aunt Donna.

There was no more discussion. The Lady had had enough of our fighting, and it was time that I go live with someone else.

In a way, I thought, "*what a piece of shit mother you are,*" but on the other hand, I felt a glimmer of hope — I could get away from these crazy people and use this as an opportunity to end up in foster care. *This* would be temporary, and it *would* be an opportunity. I just had to be strategic. I did not want to stay with my aunt and uncle; I wanted to find a new home — *my first real, safe, loving home.* I needed a strategy.

Refugee

As I prepared to pack my belongings and be banished from my childhood home, I allowed myself one final panoramic view of my bedroom — from my desk with its lamp perfectly placed in the corner and the bulletin board above, then the closet door, the first window, the freestanding mirror on its pedestal (where I loved to sit and do my makeup), then the TV on its small shelf with Beanie Babies peeking out, my chest of drawers filled with old dance costumes, the second window, my bed against the wall (with two tissue-paper flowers curled around the headboard posts), a nightstand with the cordless phone, and the dresser with an attached mirror and a meticulous arrangement of picture frames on its surface. This was the last time I would have my stuff.

The Wall of Dreams in my bedroom on Birchcroft Road

I packed two trash bags — one with clothes and shoes, and the other with my favorite possessions ... CDs, picture frames, gifts from friends, and things to hang on my walls. In my room, I had my "wall of dreams," which included magazine clippings of quotes and pictures and other miscellaneous items that gave me hope of getting out one day, hopefully before the age of 18. Time was running out.

The Lady brought me to my grandmother's house first, I guess as a punishing chamber, while she made the call to her brother that they could come pick up her "horrible daughter." I was the devil, you know. I was so misbehaved "she should have just called juvenile hall." That seemed like a great option too — I welcomed any opportunity to get out, with my preferences as follows:

1. Foster care

2. Adopted by someone, hopefully a friend's parents

3. Literally ANYWHERE.

It was a Saturday, conveniently during our February school break. This was a week I had planned on not being at home at all, and that came true, just not in the way I had envisioned.

I barely knew my aunt and uncle, but I didn't come off as a bad kid, so it was odd to me how much they enjoyed being so cold. It was as if they'd agreed to help "scare me straight." This was before the invention of cellphones and laptops. I had nowhere to go and nothing to do, so I stayed in my room and read. The room was sterile — ivory walls, brown trim, and worn wood floors. There was an uncomfortable bed and a dresser. I think they give you more in prison. I had to cross the hall to use the bathroom, which was right off their bedroom. The house was an old Victorian and it lacked insulation. Other than that, it was lonely and deathly quiet. I still get the same sour pain in the pit of my stomach when I think about sitting in that room, with nothing but a bed, blank walls, and silence. My very own prison cell. My self-esteem took a hit in silence, so I craved more noise now. Usually, I slept with my stereo or television on, but I didn't have those here. I felt so alone. Somewhat safer, perhaps, but forgotten, abandoned, and alone.

I still get the same sour pain in the pit of my stomach when I think about sitting in that room, with nothing but a bed, blank walls, and silence.

There was nothing like adding two more adults to the list of those who didn't believe me, didn't listen to me, didn't love me, and didn't treat me with love and compassion. Why was it so hard, in my world, to find someone who would treat me differently than this? I kept thinking about what happened and wondering: *Why was no one punishing my brother?* I pictured him sitting in front of the television, watching Big Daddy for the 100th time (or playing *Mario* on Nintendo), with Pepsi cans and Reese's Peanut Butter Cup wrappers surrounding him, with my sister following him around, reciting all the movie lines. I pictured him jumping on the trampoline and playing basketball with his friends. *Was anyone thinking about me?*

Waiting for Nana ... or Someone

In my old life, I was used to being on the phone almost every minute that I was inside my room. Here, I had restrictions on the length of my phone calls and I had restrictions on just about everything. I had to eat what they were cooking for dinner, which meant I didn't eat much (or at all). I wasn't allowed to nap. And I wasn't allowed to hang anything on the walls, so my "wall of dreams" stayed packed up in the trash bag. Man, I felt that metaphor. I was treated like a felon, because I was the black sheep child — the oldest, the one with the attitude, the one who neither parent wanted, and these people, it seemed, didn't want me either.

> I had to eat what they were cooking for dinner, which meant I didn't eat much (or at all). I wasn't allowed to nap. And I wasn't allowed to hang anything on the walls, so my "wall of dreams" stayed packed up in the trash bag. Man, I felt that metaphor.

The first night that I was with my aunt and uncle, they cooked pork chops with an orange marmalade glaze. I told them I didn't eat pork. Here I was, sitting at the table all night again (someone else's table this time), not eating. Were the porkchop punishments hereditary? *How could I even be hungry? The emptiness I felt was something else and nothing at all like hunger.*

I'm guessing the adults were using their unrestricted telephone time to talk about what to do with me and to share details about my hunger strike and my overall lack of compliance. Because the next day, my grandmother picked me up and took me grocery shopping. We got simple foods I liked and knew how to prepare, like applesauce, microwaveable tortellini, peanut butter and jelly, etc. Looking back, I think she knew I didn't belong there and at least she cared that I wasn't eating. She was a harsh critic, but she did have a heart.

We called her Nana (pronounced nah-nah), but my cousins called her Hunny-Bunny. Nana was the mother to The Lady and to six other kids, who were my aunts and uncles. Those seven offspring led to 17 of us grandchildren. Even though most of my cousins called our grandmother "Hunny

Bunny," I was too afraid to call her that. I was actually a little bit scared of her in general. She was strict — Catholic strict. Nana had been a nun in her younger years and now she went to church several days a week, where she was always showing up early and staying late. When I was little, sometimes we spent the night at Nana's. I didn't like to sleep over on Saturdays because that meant for an early Sunday morning with rosary beads and eating that cardboard chip for communion.

Nana was short and getting shorter. The more she shrunk, the more comical and dangerous her lack of statue seemed to be. With her black curly hair, which hugged the top of her head and sat on top of her glasses, she disappeared behind the steering wheel of her car, so small that you could barely see her through the windshield of her Buick. She would often have us at her apartment. On days when we spent time at the local "summer camp," she would make us pancakes with the just-add-water mix. When she had us for the full summer days, she groomed me into being obsessive about cleaning — eventually outright suffering from obsessive-compulsive disorder (OCD), just like her. She taught me to scrub floors on my hands and knees "because mops were not good enough." And her bell collection, which was precious and always dusty, required individual dipping sessions in the vinegar-and-water blend. She taught me how to always vacuum underneath the couch cushions, and she swapped out her window valances and bedding by the seasons. "Time for the summer comforter!" When it was my cousin Kim and me sleeping over, Nana would make us give her foot massages with Vaseline. I would cringe, keeping my eyes shut while dreaming about that vanilla and chocolate "hoodsie cup" stash in the freezer. I mean, she did have a lot of candy dishes, which was kind of cool. She liked sugar as much as she liked a clean apartment. She used to keep the special thin mints (disc-shaped creamy mint chocolates with frosted flowers on them, the likes of which I have never seen again) in the dish on her dresser, just for me.

So when I found myself banished from my abusive home at 16, Nana and I had a long history. After all those cleaning sessions and foot rubs, you would think she'd be my advocate and get me the hell out of there. I mean, why wouldn't she take me in?

Several days had passed since I was taken to live with my aunt and uncle, and I knew I would have to explain it to my friends when it was time to go back to school the following week. So I had called all my friends and told them I had moved to Clinton (about 20 minutes away from Leominster) and that I was going to switch schools. I cried during every conversation. My friends were shocked. I was embarrassed. It was hard for me to tell them my "mom" got rid of me. I also could not go into detail about the fight with my brother, because that didn't fit my image. How could I explain what was happening to me? It was easier to keep everything a secret; that way, I could keep pretending, when I was at school, that my life was perfect. Plus, I knew that my friends just wouldn't understand.

On Sunday morning, eight days after I was made out to be a mirror-breaking felon and given away to my aunt and uncle, The Lady called and asked to speak with me on the phone. Of course, I didn't want to talk to her, but again, that wasn't my choice. I was forced to take the phone. She told me I could come home. I remained silent. I didn't want to come "home." This was my way out — even if I was missing my friends, losing my extracurricular activities, and didn't have my room or the woods as my private sanctuaries anymore. I reminded her that she told me this was a permanent move — that she said I would be switching schools. She said she wanted me to learn a lesson. The conversation ended with yet another fight. I was told I was being brought back to live with my siblings that afternoon.

I repacked my two trash bags and my dreams, as I was now even further away from making it into the hands of a foster family. One step forward, two steps back. I thought I had seen a glimmer of light, but then it disappeared into darkness, while this lady controlled me back into her power, where I would be her victim, who fed her illness of being in control of something. She did not *want* me back, but her illness needed to have me there. My dad, in hospice at this point, likely had no idea what was happening at home. Nana didn't intervene, nor did anyone else. There was no one willing to save me.

So I returned to her domestic prison, where she would be standing outside my cell, with her uniform and a straight, cold face as I walked by her, feeling powerless. But I refused to become hopeless. I was too stubborn to give up.

Unfound

You don't fear me.
You can't feel me.
You can't hear me underground.
I am fighting.
I am trying.
I am everywhere around.
But when you surface,
you make me nervous,
and I become unfound.

RUN, Hide, Fight

RUN

I held my breath as I entered the house and ran from the front door, up the stairs, and to my room — clutching the two black trash bags. The cigarette smell was pervasive.

The first door at the top of the stairs was the bathroom, then to the left was my parent's room (where only my dad ever slept), my room, and then my brother's room, which later became my sister's room. I had to pass two open doors to get to mine.

My door was always shut. A "no smoking" sign faced the hallway, and I kept a Lysol can on the desk inside, an immediate grab upon entering. A rice-filled draft stopper became a smoke stopper to go under the door. I remember running to the windows, opening them both for a cross-breeze to cleanse the air. This routine became part of my OCD ritual — where I counted how many seconds it would take, as my body filled with anxiety and I tried to be faster each time.

Both of my parents smoked cigarettes. They also drank way too much coffee. I always hated these smells. I felt suffocated and I was sure I could feel the toxins entering my body. Anywhere I went, if I smelled smoke or coffee,

I smelled them — those people who had made my life such hell. The Lady stopped at these two addictions (cigarettes and coffee), but my dad added a third with his alcohol (Miller Lite, a third smell that I'm sure would repulse me if I were to encounter it again). When I think about my childhood, I can still picture the coffee pot on the Formica counter, making that gurgling noise, from morning until night. To this day, I have never touched any of these substances — smokes, coffee, or booze. The smells alone send me right back. And I don't ever want to go back.

I tried using my research on secondhand smoke to get my parents to quit. I tried dumping their cigarettes down the toilet; I tried hiding them; and I even tried explaining the financial side of this nasty habit. We had *no money* for the mortgage and *no money for groceries*, but we had $50 a day for cigarettes and $20 a day for beer. I was never great at math, but it didn't take a genius to figure out this equation. I knew that without these addictions, I would not need to buy my own shampoo or go to my friends' houses to eat. But the behavior would not stop. I always felt my parents were selfish for choosing their addictions over us. No matter how much I begged, they never tried to quit, and I knew they didn't love us like other parents loved their children.

> I always felt my parents were selfish for choosing their addictions over us. No matter how much I begged, they never tried to quit, and I knew they didn't love us like other parents loved their children.

They were each smoking three packs a day and the worst part was that they smoked inside the house and inside the car. Weekends were the worst because they were *both* home. I spent a lot of time not home or alone, in my room with the door shut or hiding in the woods. I snuck around opening windows when they weren't looking, and I was always spraying that yellow can of Lysol. I was constantly being screamed at for wasting the heat and air conditioning when I opened the windows. Their famous line was, "Do you want to pay the electric bill?"

I can't breathe. I can't fucking breathe!!!

In the car, I would stick my head out the window. Being in the car was some-thing I dreaded and hated more than any other experience. I remember when The Lady had taken a cake-baking class and decided to make an angel food cake for my cousin's birthday. The cake was layered with Cool Whip frosting with pineapples and cherries on the top. The Lady made me hold it in the back seat, without a cover or tinfoil. We had about a half-hour drive to the next town over, which meant I had to survive four cigarettes. The Lady and my dad would smoke at the same time. I would go back and forth between sticking my head out the window and filling my lungs with fresh air, then holding my breath inside the car until my breath ran out. I would get headaches from the lack of oxygen — pain that was self-inflicted, yet still better than inhaling poison.

They used their respective windows to flick the ashes off their burning ciga-rettes and I was trapped behind them, the cigarette ashes flying to the back seat and landing on top of the cake, melting down into the fluffy, white Cool Whip. It was the most disgusting thing I had ever seen. At the party, I told everyone not to eat the cake.

Hide

At "home," there was no inside voice — that quiet, respectful, even-keeled conversation volume that was used in other people's houses. There was only screaming, yelling, and the silence of fear. There was running, hiding, and fighting.

I kept a "101 Dalmatians" suitcase permanently packed under my bed. One day, I was going to need it when the cops came and took us away. I tried running away to different friends' houses many times. Sometimes my friends' parents would drive by me — walking on the main roads with my suitcase and they insisted on taking me back home. Other times, after so many consecutive sleepovers, they'd drop me off, never realizing why I never asked to go home, or why my mom didn't call them to check in on me, to offer them money for feeding me, or to see if I was alive. Down deep, I think everyone knew what kind of life I might be living. But in those days, everyone "minded their own business."

When running didn't work, I would hide. I once hid in the dirty laundry basket inside the bathroom closet. I remember my brother took a shower and I was so nervous that he would realize I was in there and tell The Lady, because then I would get in trouble, but only because I was being noticed.

My brother never did see me because my head was covered by dirty towels and I was holding my breath when he opened the door to add his towel to the top of the pile. I slept in the closet until the next day when I got too hungry. No one even realized I was missing. If I stayed quiet enough, no one knew I was alive. My life seemed much easier that way.

I would try every opportunity to not be home. In my later high school years, I would sneak out a lot. I never did anything "bad" (I was a shockingly well-adjusted kid for one who came from such dysfunction); I just didn't want to be in that freaking house, around those freaking people. I totally pulled the whole "pillows under your comforter" trick, making it look like I was sleeping. That one worked, it appeared. By this time, The Lady was a widow and was even more checked out than before. Whether she actually checked my bed when I was missing or not, I do not know.

I believe it was my junior year when I left a note saying I was sleeping at one friend's house, and The Lady actually called to check that morning when she got back from working her night shift. She did some investigating, which led to her standing at the doorstep of my friend's boyfriend's house in her correctional officer's uniform — determined to find me somewhere other than where I had indicated I'd gone. That was not an enjoyable ride home … although I was pleasantly shocked that she had actually come looking for me. It depended on her mood — and when she wanted and needed control over me — which, of course, was at her convenience.

The older I got, the worse my attitude was and when I opened my big mouth, she would notice me. That usually did *not* work out in my favor. My hate for her grew so strong that I had a hard time holding back on subjects like how bad of a mother I thought she was. She grounded me for my entire freshman year of high school for giving her attitude. I had no phone or TV and I couldn't leave the house unless I was going to school or dance. I would walk around the block after the bus dropped me off and leave notes in my friend Mike's mailbox, because then I had something to do while sitting in my room alone — look out the window and wait for his delivery, tell The

Lady I was checking the mail, and then I could write back. The excitement was real, and so was her control.

Of course, there were different degrees of escalation for her anger. If I made her mad, she would escalate up her ladder of retaliation, which included everything from yelling to screaming, kicking me out (until she realized this was what I wanted), taking away my cordless phone, forcing me to stay home (which she knew was the worst punishment), throwing things at me, or turning into an absolute monster — physical in her torture and retribution.

I was good at playing tough and, for the most part, I *was* tough. I was a good actor — acting like her actions and words didn't faze me. I had this cocky little attitude, like *"go ahead and try me, bitch."* The way she treated me affected me, but because I was a professional at closing off my emotions, I didn't have much left to lose. The impact of her cruelty and indifference could be measured, when I was young, in my low self-esteem. It wasn't until I was an adult that a lifetime of abuse and neglect took its full toll. When it did, it hit me like a projectile that came crashing through the windshield, while the glass shattered and reopened decades of wounds.

But when I was in it — in that house full of torment and terror — I didn't have time to tend to my wounds. I just kept fighting. There was one night when The Lady was getting ready for work. I came up the blue carpeted stairs, smelling that famous combo of hairspray and cigarette smoke, while listening to the bubbling coffee pot and seeing her put makeup on … a rarity. I walked into my room and she instigated an argument, as if for sport — as if the mere sight of me was cause for fury. My room was my sanctuary; it was quiet, clean, and safe in there. I followed my usual ritual and was opening my window when …

BANG!

My bedroom door flew open and slammed into the wall, and she came running through, with a lit cigarette. In my mind, my room was a "no smoking" zone and she knew they were not allowed; in her mind, this was her house and I was an uppity little bitch. I started screaming, running to my bed to go under the blankets. She pulled my hair to pull me closer to her and began blowing smoke in my face.

I closed my eyes, held my breath, and kicked her off me. The thick gray smoke filled my room, and suddenly I was running around screaming and hyperventilating. She walked away as quickly as she'd pounced. Once she left for work, I couldn't sleep. I went through two cans of Lysol and slept with my head by the open window.

Fight

It was a Saturday Halloween — my favorite holiday and on the perfect day of the week. I loved dressing up as something both random and creative, where I could make my own costume and, of course, collect and trade candy.

I didn't care for the scary costumes or the standard array of vampire, witch, and grim reaper. I had designed and created costumes ranging from a Raisinets, a banana, a bar of Zest soap, a red Crayola crayon, and Snap, Crackle and Pop from the Rice Krispies.

In Massachusetts, some Halloweens were snow covered, which did not always align with the costume designs. Some were mild, which made for the best trick-or-treating. This particular year, the weather was mild, the calm before the storm.

I think I was 16 years old on this Halloween. That would have made my sister 9 and the perfect age for trick-or-treating. My brother, 15, was also dressing up to take my sister around the neighborhood. We always went by ourselves. As was the case in our everyday lives, we participated without supervision.

I was working at Subway, the sandwich shop we all know and love. I was a "sandwich artist" and I loved my job. This was possibly my first Halloween working instead of being with my friends, and I wanted to use my 30-minute lunch break to go home and see my sister before she went out in her costume. This gave me 13 minutes to drive home, 13 minutes to drive back, and only four minutes to see my sister. I was convinced I could make it.

This time, I *walked* in the door instead of running, feeling the immediate darkness just momentarily until I lit up with delight, looking to the right and seeing my siblings standing in their costumes in the living room. They were both vampires, with white faces, plastic fangs, and blood stains dripping from their eyes. The Lady heard me come in. Immediately, I knew I should have been quieter.

She started yelling. I can never remember the cause. *Three minutes left.*

I ran up the stairs, through the door with the "no smoking" sign, grabbed the Lysol, shoved the draft stopper under, sprayed and opened the windows. *Two minutes left.*

My door slammed opened and hit the wall. The Lady was screaming as she grabbed the white wire shoe rack and threw it at me across the room. *One minute left.*

Time slowed as she came after me, grabbing my hair to pull me onto the carpet, swinging wildly, throwing punches, and screaming all of her favorite lines. *I was late.*

"You're a bitch!!!"

"Rot in hell, Danielle!!! You should never have come home!!!"

I got up off the floor after pulling her hair to gain time. She kept pulling at my clothes and swinging her arms. I wanted to punch back, but once I looked at her face, I couldn't do it. I was looking down at her, her thick frizzy, black dyed hair was covering her face and her thin eyes were filled with unprecedented rage and suffering.

I let her hit me while I stood there, looking down and feeling sorry for her. I could not hit her back. I remember thinking, *"you can't hit your mom ..."* even though I did not love her.

I wondered what was wrong with her. I still wonder.

I have, in fact, spent a lot of time trying to figure out how she became the woman I knew her to be. I keep coming back to two traumatic experiences she mentioned to me. She said that she had three miscarriages before I was born and that when she was pregnant with me, an inmate in the prison attempted to stab her pregnant stomach. I believe the knife punctured her skin, but I am not positive on any other details. She did mention she always wanted a lot of children. I remember standing in front of her dresser while she was getting ready for work and hearing these words that left me staring and thinking, "*WHY? What happened then? You actually wanted us?*"

I never understood why she would want more children, when she didn't love the ones she had. Of course, I have hypotheses, but I will never know. My mind used to race, wondering when I would know the answer. One of my theories is that the miscarriages — coupled with my dad's alcoholism — changed her psyche and broke her in some way. Maybe she hated her job that much; she did complain about it. Maybe she wanted to have a lot of children so she could give what she never received — love. Maybe it was a way to cover and heal from her emptiness and loneliness. *Maybe* if she had a lot of kids, she would have enough kids to love her back.

Wolf Cry

If you are known for lying,
do not bother telling the truth,
because no one will ever believe you.
If you are known for telling the truth,
but no one is willing to face it,
no one will ever listen.

4

The Girl Who Cried Wolf

I was sprinting down the hill and, for the first time, I had gained some distance out ahead of my brother. I was winning the race; maybe I would be safe. I could barely see my feet, but I felt them hitting the pavement at a rapid speed, as the trees whipped past my peripheral, looking like an impressionist painting. The air was finally cool, but my heart was beating so fast that I was sweating through my shirt. Thank god my hair was tied back tightly — I couldn't let it slow me down. I was ahead and I felt faster than ever before, until I heard a baby crying. I stopped immediately and looked back. There was my baby sister, alone, in her car seat in the middle of the road.

The nightmares were all the same. I was being chased. It was dark and I was running down Birchcroft Road. Sometimes I felt fast, because in the darkness I felt like I was flying, but I wouldn't be able to see. Sometimes I *was* able to see, but my legs stopped working. However the nightmares played out, I was never able to scream. I would keep trying, straining my vocal cords, squeezing my eyes in a desperate effort to gain volume, but my voice was never there. I was screaming in silence.

The nightmares were all the same. I was being chased.
It was dark and I was running down Birchcroft Road.

Gaining a Sister, Losing a Home

I am not sure why, but every time my dad tucked me in as a young girl, he would tell me the tale of *The Girl Who Cried Wolf* — inspired by Aesop's 1867 Greek fable, *The Boy Who Cried Wolf*, but he changed the pronoun to make it more relatable. Or more chilling.

For whatever reason, I loved the moral of this story. No matter how many times he told it, I still requested it each night he walked me up the stairs, as I got into my bed and he shut off the lights.

He told:

> *There was a young shepherd girl who lived in the valley. Her days tending sheep proved to be quiet, so she thought of a way to create some excitement. She yelled, "Wolf! Wolf!" The villagers came running out. They didn't see a wolf, but they spent time with her, engaging in conversation and giving her the attention she sought. A few days later, the girl cried again, "Wolf! Wolf!" The villagers came running, but still, no wolf. They left her to her work tending the sheep. Shortly after her second cry, a wolf came out of the forest. The girl cried louder than ever before, "Wolf! Wolf!" but no one came. The wolf ate all the sheep! The girl was weeping because no one came to help her, but they no longer believed her cry.*

I remember when my sister was born. I was 7 and my brother was 6. I remember it clearly — walking into the white hospital room, with the daylight streaming in from the window and shining down on this baby with fuzzy black hair. She was perfectly wrapped up, like a present — she wouldn't be for The Lady, but she would be for me.

I don't remember The Lady taking care of her much. I was the one changing her diapers and making her bottles. I held her, a lot. I dressed her, combed her hair, and put her clothes away. For years prior to my little sister's birth, I had a toy baby doll — a Waterbabies brand doll. To me, my doll felt like a real baby — she had weight to her, with a hole in her mouth for a bottle and a hole down below to pee. My sister was my real "waterbaby" — she felt real, looked real, and believe me, her cry was real. For some reason, at 7 years old, I felt ready to take care of her.

Her hair began to lighten and her eyes stayed bright blue. Her skin was fair and her head round, just like Dad's. She looked like a linebacker in baby form — thick, wide, and dense. Her leg rolls rippled all the way down to her feet, which were always shoeless, sockless, and running around fast. She was rarely wearing more than a diaper and she was always sucking on a NUK pacifier, which we affectionately called her "nookie."

We often joked that my sister was raised by the wolves. We did not have a nanny or a babysitter, my sister was never in a formal daycare, and — truth be told — she barely had parents. Dad left by 5:30 each morning to cross the Massachusetts state border to Connecticut, and The Lady worked 11:00 p.m. to 7:00 a.m. at the prison, with over an hour commute each way. My brother and I left for school early each morning, before The Lady got home, leaving our baby sister with a neighbor. Because The Lady worked nights, she would sleep all day while we were at school. My sister was there, free-roaming with a full, dirty diaper trailing behind her, slowing her down. I imagine her like a duckling falling behind the rest of the flock or a stray, forgotten sheep — maybe one of those sheep in *The Girl Who Cried Wolf* — all while The Lady slept, oblivious to the baby, on the brown couch.

 We often joked that my sister was raised by the wolves. We did not have a nanny or a babysitter, my sister was never in a formal daycare, and — truth be told — she barely had parents.

Before my sister's birth came financial ruin and a move. And it all set off a cascade of events that would characterize the rest of my childhood. I guess after we went bankrupt and my parents blamed it on the cost of daycare, those options were over — even though there was now a new baby who needed care. I remember those days before my sister's birth, when my brother and I were at two different home daycares — one with a scary woman named Cindy. Cindy hit us. Knowing this, The Lady picked us up and never brought us back. This may have been the only time she protected us; I guess she thought abuse *outside* the family was unacceptable. It was not long after that when we lost our house, leaving Gove's Farm next door, losing our tractor rides and perfectly manicured backyard. There had been something pure and priceless about living next door to a farm. The smell of manure meant that we would see crops soon. Crops meant tractor rides for my brother and me. Across the busy street was the "Home of Johnny Appleseed" sign and off in the distance was the large red building that housed the best birthday party venue, Roll On America. Oh, how we had loved roller skating! We were forced to leave all this behind, having to rent a much smaller home on Smith Street, with just one bathroom for our family of five.

We lived on Smith Street for two years — getting me through kindergarten and first grade, just in time to switch schools for second grade. I remember my parents telling me that bankruptcy lasted seven years and that we could not buy a house for a while because they had no credit. The word "credit" has been part of my vocabulary since I was five years old. I didn't understand what it was, but I knew that not having it was bad.

The word "credit" has been part of my vocabulary since I was five years old. I didn't understand what it was, but I knew that not having it was bad.

On Smith Street, we had great neighbors on the right side — a sweet mom named Coco, her husband John (who worked all the time), and their two daughters, Brianna and Courtney. We would go to Coco's in the mornings before school, carrying my sister in a car seat that had a handle. Coco had a vibrant and bubbly personality just like her name. Her real name was Colleen, but Coco fit her. She had shoulder-length curly hair and wore gold hoop earrings. She was a hairdresser and I remember her teaching me how to braid hair on one of those fake heads. Coco would get us on the bus and my baby sister would go back home to stay in the crib while The Lady slept.

I will never forget my first sleepover with Brianna. I had bunk beds (and no little sister yet to share them with) and I loved the thrill of taking the top because a friend was visiting. It was 3:00 a.m. when Brianna knocked on the bottom of my bunk above her. She said she did not feel good and she was scared. I was upset she wanted to go back home, but I walked her to her door in the dark morning hours, we woke Coco, and I came back inside to go back to sleep.

An hour later, all hell broke loose. We were robbed. The Lady heard something out in the kitchen and went out there a few times, but didn't think to look under the kitchen table, where the intruders were hiding. My dad, who encountered the intruders, took off down the street, chasing the three men with a baseball bat. He never caught them, but they did drop our TVs, VCR, and other stolen items in a backyard down the street. Ours had been the last robbery in a string of home invasions on our street that night. The only reason the robbers were able to get in to our house so easily was because our door was left unlocked after Brianna went home. She had been right — something was wrong and it was a night for being scared.

The House on Birchcroft Road

It was time to move and thank goodness we were able to buy a house again. I remember looking at it with the realtor and I ran around proclaiming that this was THE house and we had to have it. I wanted the biggest room with two windows, well, because I was the oldest and I was a girl, so I needed more room. And there were three bathrooms! The yard was perfect for running, the woods looked perfect for exploring, and the neighborhood was full of kids. This was one of the first times, as I child, that I felt full of hope and joy.

The house on Birchcroft Road sat around the bend, where colonial-style and Cape Cod-inspired houses lined the street, all with vinyl siding, shutters, and large yards. Our house was tan with brown shutters, a two-story colonial with a room that jutted out on the left side, where the side yard lay flat and empty, ready for capture-the-flag and football games. It had a large aspen tree on the right side of the front yard — by the neighboring white colonial with black shutters. On the left side was a crab apple tree by the blue Cape Cod, also with black shutters. The driveway was steep, sloping down to the garage that tucked below the house and hung off the creepy basement.

My initial idea of this house was far better than it ended up being. The house was not the issue, but the people in it brought too much darkness. The darkness manifested dread, fear, anger, violence, and anxiety, and it triggered obsessions that spiraled in different directions for each of us. My dad drank more. The Lady slept more. My brother hit more. I developed OCD.

My initial idea of this house was far better than it ended up being. The house was not the issue, but the people in it brought too much darkness.

My sister, innocent in so many ways, was at the center of the chaos. After school, I would walk in the door (which I could barely open because the floor was covered in toys) to find my sister shirtless, with a dirty diaper. All I had to do was follow the trail of mess to see what she did that day. I would quickly run upstairs and assess the damage in my room. I would have complete meltdowns and then spend hours getting everything perfect again. We owned buckets full of McDonald's Happy Meal toys, which she would dump as if there was treasure at the bottom. My anxiety would build as I got on the school bus. I hated going home. I hated messes and I hated finding my room and my things destroyed, seeing blue eye shadow all over her face and lipstick in her hair. The Lady would sometimes have her face covered in Sharpie marker doodles. She didn't wake up for anything.

I became obsessive compulsive, but without some of the most common OCD behaviors, like ticks, hand washing, or making sure things were unplugged. I had to have everything in my room perfect. Once I finally got my sister in her own room and my brother moved into the basement, no one was allowed in and no one could touch anything. My picture frames were harmoniously aligned and angled on top of my dresser, while my little porcelain tea party set was always display-ready (but never used) sitting on top of the mirrored tray. I had to obsessively clean the house, otherwise I couldn't go to bed. Sometimes I would circle the vacuum around the same rooms two or three times until I felt like I had picked up all the dirt. They all called me crazy, and I assumed I was.

I had developed counting rituals, but never told anyone about them because I was embarrassed. I would count the same areas in my room over and over.

I would connect invisible lines from one object to another and associate a number with an object. For example, I would start at the light switch and that was number 1, then I would draw an invisible line to my desk, which was number 2, and then over to my TV which was number 3. I often traced the lines in my ceiling with my eyes, over and over and over.

They all called me crazy, and I assumed I was.

There was a rule in our house: If I wanted to go anywhere, I had to take my sister. I assumed it was because The Lady didn't want to watch her. I did her hair in the morning, picked out her outfits, and made sure she had breakfast. As much as I loved these maternal responsibilities, I gained resentment over time.

One day, I sat her in my desk chair, in front of the dresser with the mirror above. Her bangs were cut straight across her forehead, always longer than they should be. The bangs brushed her long eyelashes, which fluttered over her bright blue eyes. Her chubby cheeks filled her pronounced cheek bones, which looked just like our dad's, but I didn't want her to feel special, because I certainly didn't feel special. I wanted to hurt her feelings because mine were hurt. Her needs overshadowed mine. I didn't want to become an adult. I didn't want to feel like I had this child to raise. She wasn't mine. I remember the following conversation distinctly:

Me: "You are the only child with blue eyes and blonde hair. I would ask Mom and Dad if you were adopted."

My sister: "Don't you remember me being born, Sissy?"

Me: "Well, I didn't actually see you coming out. They could have easily adopted you in the hospital."

My sister: "I look just like Dad though. Everyone says I look just like Dad."

Me: "You are seven years younger than me. You were adopted. If you ask them, they will probably lie to you, but it makes sense if you think about it."

This was the only lie I remember telling. I really didn't like to lie and I wasn't particularly good at it. But the older I got, the more annoying she got. The more annoying she got, the more lies she told, because that was her newest obsession (once she realized she could get attention by lying). The more lies she told, the worse our relationship got.

If only our dad had a voice left to tell my favorite story. The girl who cried wolf kept crying. And I learned to stop listening.

Just Like Them

These emotions,
fast approaching,
boil at the surface.
Always a quick release.
So deep I still don't see me.
An emotion as clear as the river,
as toxic as the sewer.
Black out, yell, scream,
I am yelling so you hear me!
I see red,
and feel shame.
These emotions make me *just like them.*
I run away fast,
escaping the herd,
to where there is no more yelling,
just the loud echo of my own thoughts
and my throbbing head.

Bullies and a Black Sheep

I walked up the hill and was just around the bend. I could see our tree in the front yard. The leaves were a bright green and the branches were full. I loved the color green. The sun was streaming through the green leaves and when I looked down, I saw a green dollar bill on the pavement. It was crumpled up, seeming like an illusion, sitting quietly at the foot of the neighbor's driveway.

I looked around. I didn't see or hear anyone, so I grabbed the dollar.

The dollar escaped my hand just as fast as I grabbed it. It was dragged down Mike's driveway on fishing line. I looked back down at the ground, trying to understand what was happening. When I looked up, a basketball hit me right in the face. I heard bursts of laughter, but I didn't need to look at their faces. My lips were throbbing. I licked my bottom lip and tasted blood.

I screamed, "Go fuck yourself! You gave me a fat lip!"

"It's OK. You have dick-sucking lips. They can't get much bigger."

I walked into the emotional darkness of that sunny day — consumed by embarrassment and anger, and with throbbing, fat lips.

Stay-at-Home Dad

Since Dad worked in commercial construction at the time of his ALS diagnosis, his failing legs became a major liability on the job site. After a few roof falls, his boss let him go and Dad was now home, all day, every day, right before my freshman year of high school. There was no big white company truck in the driveway. There was now one car and only one working parent. We were suddenly reliant financially on the "parent" with the smaller income — who worked the night shift and slept during the day, missing every phone call from the school nurse when her children were sick.

I remember when my dad tried to do my laundry. It was the answer to my prayers — *finally, a laundry service!* — until he questioned my underwear selection, which was extremely embarrassing because I had just bought my first three thongs. My bubble butt came just in time for high school and I could *not* have underwear lines showing through my jeans.

I went to go grab my new rhinestone-studded shirt for the second day of school, after having worn a dress the previous day (because I *always* wore a dress on the first day of school). I picked up the shirt and immediately realized it looked like it was purchased for my younger sister. It had shrunken at least two sizes! I looked at my dad, about to yell at him for ruining my brand-new shirt, but once I opened my mouth and looked toward him, I was struck silent by the gravity of his situation. He was sicker today than yesterday, alone, and doing laundry instead of construction. He had a debilitating, degenerative disease without a cure and without hope. I could not say a word. This was all he had to do now. The only thing he could still do was his kids' laundry.

For my dad, domestic duties and laundry days didn't last long, as the wheelchair days approached and his vocal cords were resting on mute. ALS was attacking every muscle, slowly and carefully. I didn't like watching a disease slowly kill someone, and it was something out of his control and not his fault — working faster than those 30-can cases of Miller Lite on his liver.

Going Through the Motions

Our house quickly became a hospital as Dad's ALS inevitably progressed. After the falls became too frequent, the ambulance fees were replaced by the cost of in-home nurses. It felt like it happened overnight. One day, I came home from school to find my little sister opening plastic Easter eggs with a random elderly man in our front yard. I went inside to ask The Lady who this man was, sort of hoping he was an adopted grandfather I wasn't aware of and that he was there to give us love and attention. She said he was part of the in-home hospice care that was provided for families with younger children. I grew up without either grandfather, both passing before I was born, so I was happy that my sister was able to borrow one, *temporarily.*

In the pool table room (or more aptly described as Dad's drinking-and-smoking room), the usual setup was a recliner in front of the television, the pool table flanking the entire center of the room and the dark wooden desk in the right corner. That desk was where the stress landed — where the bills were supposed to be paid. A sliding door opened off the back of the room and led onto the deck, which overlooked the dog tied between two trees and the small hill that was up-wind from the above-ground pool. The carpet was light beige and the walls ivory, both darkened by the cigarette smoke. The pool table had not been used since Dad fell while mopping the kitchen floor and ended up with a head full of stitches. His legs never recovered after that, so the pool table stayed covered in dumped piles of laundry (because, at our house, no task was ever completed).

Now, there was a hospital bed that replaced the recliner. And there were breathing machines, wheelchairs, and hospital equipment, but my parents never got rid of the pool table. There was no bath or shower downstairs, so I am not sure how they were bathing him. I assume he had a disability insurance policy that was covering this, because we didn't have money for groceries, never mind this personal hospital operation — especially now, on one income. I did not ask questions and I tried not to look. I just came home less and less, living in the safety of denial.

The progression of my dad's illness was a trauma in and of itself, but it also brought other harsh memories and realities into stark focus. I remember that when I was perhaps 8 years old, I was beginning to make friends in our new neighborhood and the two sisters up the street came for a sleepover.

The next day, I walked them home and their mom complained that their clothes smelled like cigarette smoke. She said I could sleep at their house from now on, but they were not allowed to stay over at my house. After that, I never let my clothes touch the top of the pool table.

The room — where we once stored laundry and eventually put my father in a hospital bed — was filled with windows, but they were never opened. The air was thick and musty like a hotel room in the smoking section. If I had to go in there, I would run in holding my breath, then run straight outside so that my lungs would be cleared. I always pictured myself having black lungs from the secondhand smoke. I never could hold my breath long underwater, so I spent extra hours in the pool, practicing laps as I pictured my lungs releasing the black soot and filling with fresh, clean air.

In our house on Birchcroft Road, the yelling was mostly directed at me. I always assumed it was because I was the oldest. My dad would yell at me for opening windows and turning up the heat in the winter, while The Lady yelled at me for simply being there. My bedroom windows were always open, truly making me a household felon in my dad's eyes. My room was below freezing during the winters, but I preferred to be cold rather than suffocate. I was always suffocating. With my door shut, the heat from the baseboard heaters would shut off. Dad always kept the heat on 64 so I would sneak and turn it up when I came home. I was *always* caught. When he *could* yell, the yelling started at the front door. If we took too long to shut the front door, his voice would send shrills down my spine. "Do you think we live in a barn??? Do you know how much our heat bill was last month???" I learned how to drown out his yell, so I could sneak a few extra seconds of that cold, fresh air before closing the door and quietly running up the stairs. The house needed oxygen and the fresh-fallen-snow air was the crispest, purest air there was.

In our house on Birchcroft Road, the yelling was mostly directed at me. I always assumed it was because I was the oldest.

In those harsh winters, it was hard to get out of bed in the morning, from leaving the covers to seeing the pitch-dark sky through snowfall, then feeling the limited hot water before walking down the street to the bus stop. Then the summers were unbearable. It was years before I had a window-unit air conditioner, so I would empty the ice maker on my comforter, then pour cups of water on top, so the ice-cold temperature would fill my comforter and it would last through the night. I thought I was on the show *Survivor*. My active imagination was often my best friend in that loveless house.

Of course, my favorite time to be home was when no one else was home. I would secretly open all the windows, spray all the Lysol, and light all the candles. My babysitting money was well spent at the mall's Yankee Candle store. After I set up the scents, I would vacuum each room two or three times, until I felt I had cleaned their filth out of every cut piece of yarn. I would take the vacuum hose and start on the left side of each stair, then run across the longest line where the tread met the riser, and then cut back in on the right side. I would repeat this process thousands of times through the years. Although it was quiet without anyone home, the vacuum became my radio. If my siblings or parents were home, the vacuum was my white noise machine. The others craved the noise while I craved the silence. I appreciated the silence just as much as I appreciated the clean carpet.

The Wrong Crowd

It was a sunny and lonely Saturday afternoon in the early 2000s, and I had walked to all my friends' houses to find out that no one was home. I had delivered papers all morning but didn't yet have my worker's permit and was desperate to find ways to pass the time. I was in that stage of childhood where there was less playing and more boredom now than ever before. I remember walking back toward our house, hunched over in disappointment as I passed my brother playing basketball in the bottom of our driveway. He was with our neighbor Mike and his posse, who became my regular bullies. Mike was the one who had spearheaded the dollar-on-the-fishing-line prank. The last time I saw Mike and his minions, they had taped funnels to their chests, running up and down the street yelling, "Hey Danielle, this will NEVER be you! Time to get a boob job!"

I quietly walked inside. The Lady was out running errands with my sister. My dad was in his wheelchair in the pool room. I kept picturing these jerks running around making fun of me for being flat-chested, but the one I hated the most, Bryan, was on my mind. I was going to get him back today.

I scanned around looking for something, but I didn't know what. I did what I *knew* how to do. I opened the fridge. I poured the tallest glass of orange juice and tiptoed outside. I hid behind the stone wall until they were facing the other direction and then I yelled, "HEY! You will never make fun of me again!" and I poured the orange juice over Bryan's head. Then I ran. He stopped coming around after that.

The very next day, a Sunday, I got a foreboding feeling. My intuition told me that something was going on with my brother. I suspected that he was following the lead of the wrong crowd, which included those jerks. They were two years older than me, and three years older than my brother, and my brother wasn't like me (stubborn, independent) — he was a follower. I had no real reason to believe I was on the right track, but something told me to check my brother's room for drugs.

I did not know what marijuana looked like, but I remember the kids in school saying it looked like oregano, a spice way too sophisticated for our pancake dinners and frozen chicken nuggets at 99 Birchcroft. I opened each drawer, wiggled my hands around the top of the dresser, went through his closet and NOTHING. I was like a police dog, a dalmatian, like the one on the front of my packed suitcase. I knew something was there, but I was missing it.

My cordless room phone rang, and I desperately picked it up on the first half ring, hoping and praying one of my friends wanted to hang out. On the tip of my tongue: "*I can be there in 10!*"

But it wasn't for me.

"Hey, is your brother there?"

"Yeah, hold on."

I screamed his name until he answered downstairs on the kitchen house phone, which was still attached to the wall.

I heard his friend ask, "Yo, can you meet me at the end of the street in 15 minutes?"

The call didn't sound innocent and I was embracing my role as amateur detective, so I stayed on the line. My intuition was burning inside my chest and I felt that dirty, grimy sensation in the pit of my stomach.

"Yeah bro, see you in a few."

The call was quick. There was a meet-up happening, but there was no explanation as to *why*.

My brother came up the stairs and I pretended I was going down the stairs, while my feet ran in place on the third stair and my little eyes peered through the railing so that I could see through the cracked opening of his wooden door. His hand reached into his dirty laundry, which was wedged between the dresser and the wall, and out came a little plastic bag that had that oregano inside.

The ONE place I didn't look — his dirty laundry.

And then it hit me: *"HOLY SHIT — my brother is a drug dealer!!!!!!"*

If I was going to be a detective, I would need to lower my standards and be willing to put my OCD aside. I acted nonchalant, walking up the stairs and asking where he was going.

"I am going to meet up with John."

"OK. When are you coming back?"

"None of your business."

I ran into the pool room, going to tattle to the silent man in a wheelchair. His blank stare made him look helpless and innocent. It was weird to see the roles reversed now.

"DAD! Your son is a DRUG DEALER!!!! Your 13-year-old son is a criminal!!! He is on a drug deal RIGHT NOW!! I cannot believe this!!! He is just like YOU — an addict! I am going to lock him out of the house! I am not living with a drug dealer!!!!"

The anticipated silence.

Oh, I wasn't done.

"I hope that you realize what this means! Your son is going to be just like you! He is not allowed back here and there is nothing you can do about it!!"

I can see myself yelling this monologue and I still feel the heartbreak. I had lost him too. My brother was gone. I locked the doors.

I couldn't stop crying and I needed to leave the house before my brother came back home and started kicking down doors. I knew if I went to my cousin Kim's house, I could do so without getting in trouble. The Lady loved to tell me I couldn't leave the house "for no reason," but visiting family always seemed a legitimate reason.

Finding My Calling

Kim was the youngest of four and her mother was my aunt, The Lady's older sister. The Lady was scary — mentally corrupt and unpredictable scary. My aunt, on the other hand, was a yeller who could send chills down your spine with the vibrations and volume of her shrill voice echoing from two floors down. At Kim's, we tried to stay in her room when her mom was home. She had a small TV in her room and we would sit on her bed with our cranberry juice and ginger ale blends. I remember the day we stumbled upon a new show on TLC called *Trading Spaces*; it was hosted by Paige Davis and it was my WTF moment. The show was based on two sets of neighbors who swapped houses, each working with an interior designer to redesign one room for one another over the course of a weekend. At the end of the weekend, the couples would have a big reveal, seeing their new-and-improved room and they were always crying tears of joy, jumping up and down, hugging everyone during this "life changing" moment. I didn't understand why people loved their homes. I didn't understand why these people were so emotional about their homes. Then I realized it is because they had a *home* — not a house, but a **home**.

I was 13 years old and I had decided what I would do for the rest of my life. I wanted to create this for people — the thing I never had, what I couldn't understand, but wanted to: a home. I wanted to be an interior designer. Kim and I continued to binge-watch reruns and *Trading Spaces* marathons. We were hooked.

Things were never the same after I returned home from hiding out with my cousin. I could feel the shift as I came to grips with the fact that I had lost two family members to addiction rather than death. It was like I could see the future for my brother. I knew this was just the beginning and I was devastated.

Facing His Mortality and My Demons

After that, my brother and I rarely spoke. We didn't even bother acknowledging each other when we passed in the high school hallways. Now, with Dad getting sicker and moving into hospice, I was "an evil bitch" because I refused to go visit someone who was dying. My family hated me for not visiting my dad, but they didn't understand. Plus, what teenager is prepared to watch a 50-year-old exhibiting all the undeniable signs of dying? I did not want to go there, so I didn't.

By this time, I had a worker's permit (I had turned 14) and I finally had real job. I was hustling to get out of the house any way I could. Sundays and holidays paid "time and a half," so I was always looking for the Sunday double. I would trade shifts, beg for shifts, and tell my bosses that I wanted to work every holiday. *Even Christmas and Easter?* Even Christmas and Easter. A Catholic town would not understand.

It was Easter Sunday, and I was disappointed to be scheduled for only one shift instead of that sought-after double. My friends were all with their families on this holy hell of a day. That meant I had to go back home.

I was in my sacred spot — my bedroom — with the door closed as I was changing out of my oversized forest green Subway polo, which smelled like a combination of baked bread and all the deli meats. I took my hair down, looking like a bird's nest, matted flat from the Subway visor and showing all the signs of the humidity that was emitted from the bread-baking machine. I lifted each foot, removed each sock, and rustled around in my "comfy clothes" drawer. It was quieter than usual, as it seemed everyone was getting ready to leave. PERFECT TIMING.

BOOM! My door was slammed open, while my brother and my half-brother tag-teamed an attack — one grabbing my legs and one grabbing my arms while lifting me in the air and running down the 13 blue carpeted stairs and out through the dark front door.

I was being kidnapped.

A rare scene it was — these two brothers, neither feeling like loyal allies but instead joined forces to be the chosen enemy. I was kicking and screaming as they threw me into the back seat and I was forced to join this psychotic blend of inhumane humans for Easter dinner ... at my dad's hospice facility. Being kidnapped to a place where people die is sort of like being forced to have a birthday party in a cemetery. I would never forgive them.

Being kidnapped to a place where people die is sort of like being forced to have a birthday party in a cemetery. I would never forgive them.

The sun was shining through the wildflowers outside in the courtyard while the inside of the building felt eerie and too quiet. There was a long table set up and Dad was at the end in his wheelchair, now with a head full of white hair, many missing teeth, and a body of mush.

We were all sitting at the same table for the first time ever. My dad in his wheelchair, The Lady, my brother (14), my sister (9), my half-brother (25) and his girlfriend, the hospice workers, and me. I felt bad for the hospice ladies — they had to work today and they had to be a part of this rare and awkward occurrence. I hoped they were getting paid time-and-a-half.

My family didn't even know how to sit at the same table for a meal. And we certainly didn't know how to talk to each other. I looked across: bully. I looked to the right: bully. I looked to the left, I looked diagonal — I didn't belong here. I was not like them. I was the sheep in *The Girl Who Cried Wolf* — the black one, all by herself, dreaming of being 18 years old and in college, free and safe and able to breathe.

Since Dad couldn't talk, the silence was just as painful as his stare, which I could feel from the end of the table, all the way to my furthest corner. I didn't want to look at him, but the stare was growing legs and running toward my eyes. It was so bothersome that I had to quickly glance, letting our eyes lock momentarily. His eyes were sad. Very sad. I knew he was sorry, and I imagined this was his nonverbal apology ... for everything.

Gypsy

I ain't got no lunch money,
but I got a Flintstone vitamin left on the counter.
'Cuz she left 3 vitamins, but lunch money only for 2.

I ain't got no lunch money,
but I got my brother's sweatpants
'cuz I don't mind sharing those.

I ain't got no lunch money,
but I have my paper route tips
filling up my plastic Pepsi bottle piggy bank.

I ain't got no lunch money,
so I became a gypsy,
beggin' for a quarter from all the boys,
learning way too early
how to get those Slim Jims and Pringles at the class store.

Lunch was really the 50-cent cafeteria cookie
that left the wax paper coated in grease …
because I was taught to buy cheap
and learned to beg to eat.
But I was never full.

6

Lunch Money

The '90s were the best years to grow up. Those '90s summers were perfect for getting your own cordless phone to talk to friends all night after being with them all day. It was the time of boy bands, girl bands, Britney Spears, and Christina Aguilera. It was the time for lip syncs, slumber party choreography, scrunchies, and roller blading birthday parties. The '90s left us on summer day cliffhangers for the MTV Total Request Live countdowns while we waited for those TGIF Friday-night shows like *Boy Meets World* and *Sabrina the Teenage Witch*. It was a fun time filled with music, dance, and friends.

As difficult as my life was, there were diversions and adventures and pockets of joy that kept me going. My friends were my salvation. We spent all our time outside, we walked everywhere, and we would shout the lyrics of TLC's "No Scrubs" down the street as we looped around the block multiple times a day. We walked to the donut shop and the ice cream shop and almost never missed the ice cream man in his refrigerated truck. We would sell lemonade outside our houses and babysit the neighborhood kids on the weekend nights to get our daily Bugs Bunny or Sponge Bob Square Pants ice cream with gumball eyeballs. Then we would use the rest of our change for those 5-cent sour Cry Babies, because they lasted longer than the eyeballs.

We had our secret path cut-throughs — the passageways we made through a stranger's or a neighbor's yard. We always met halfway, whether that was in the woods, in someone's yard, or on the street. I had a halfway meetup with each friend who was close enough to get to by foot. We built forts and crossed bridges along the creek, after swinging across on the rope swing. We made out with boys behind rocks in the woods while our friends counted how many Mississippis. We pool-hopped, trampoline-bopped, and kicked it by the movie theatre for co-ed rendezvous. There were days we even walked to our middle school and the Pop Warner field, because it gave us something to do. Having a destination for a long walk gave us important plans — it gave us somewhere to be so we weren't sitting at home bored out of our minds (or in harm's way).

Somewhere around the age of 10 or 11, I remember my dad could still walk and he was still working when The Lady planned a spontaneous and irresponsible pool purchase. I remember her telling us that a local pool company was running a summer special where you could buy a 24-foot diameter above-ground pool for $1,200. She knew our dad would say no, so while he was at work, the pool company came and leveled the dirt and assembled the pool. We had a running hose draped over the edge when Dad pulled into the driveway that evening. I don't remember him being upset at all but that's probably because, when he got out of his truck, he had three empty beer cans and a new case of Miller Lite. We begged him to get in the water with us. He grabbed a cold one and entered the pool with a smile on his face.

The Lady had done similar things before. At that point in my life, my sister and I still shared a room and we didn't have a dresser. The Lady went to MCM Furniture and put our bedroom set on layaway, which was the same way she did our Christmases. We "financed" everything. Our dad never knew, and I don't know when or how he found out. One time, she came home and told us she went to Kmart and put our school clothes on layaway. I was becoming a pre-teen and wearing Kmart clothes was social suicide. I remember standing in the pool room, throwing a tantrum that she tried to pick out clothes for me and that she had to get them at freaking Kmart!!!

"Return those clothes or I won't wear them! You don't even know what I like! You DON'T KNOW ME! I will buy my own clothes. The name-brand clothes are the same prices as Kmart when you shop the clearance racks. Did you even know that? You aren't even saving money! You are so stupid for doing this. I am NOT wearing those ugly, stupid clothes!"

I was an unspoiled but ungrateful, pre-teen bitch. Screaming at my mother accomplished nothing, but it was cathartic. I liked being mean to her because she was mean to me.

I was an unspoiled but ungrateful, pre-teen bitch. Screaming at my mother accomplished nothing, but it was cathartic. I liked being mean to her because she was mean to me.

As excited as I was about having a pool during those hot summers, I was old enough to hear my parents complain about money and how much everything cost. "The electric bill was high this month." "How did you go through ANOTHER pair of football cleats?" "We can't afford a babysitter so you can watch your sister." "There's no food because you ate it too quickly; you need to make it last longer." "Haircuts are too expensive." Instead of celebrating like my siblings, I was concerned about how this was going to work … because I knew we didn't have money for a pool.

The next summer sucked the celebration out of the blue water and traded it in for a cloudy, green algae. The Lady was regretting her pool purchase, but I regretted it more because it was embarrassing to have a green pool. It was annoying to listen to the complaints about the cost of chlorine and the increased electric bill from the pool pump. We were not allowed to keep the pump on during our summer days at home and definitely not overnight. We weren't allowed to run the pool vacuum every day either, even though it needed it because the trees overhung the water, leaving a constant mess. The pool was a lot of work and for someone with OCD, it was just too much. I wouldn't swim in that water if it wasn't crystal clear — without any bugs, dirt, or leaves — so now I was just more embarrassed about my house and more overwhelmed with something *else* that was always a mess.

Extra! Extra! Read All About It

I was 12 when The Lady told me I needed to get a job. I had some choice words for her, which included me explaining that I couldn't get a job without a worker's permit. I believe I also recited classic pre-teen lines about how she was taking away my childhood and turning me into a slave. Her response was a two-word phrase that changed the course of the rest of my life: paper route. *You mean there's a loophole to child labor?* Apparently so.

My brother was 11 and he became my business partner. I was desperate to not be in this alone, and he was lucky I didn't have time to do a background check.

In 1999, paper routes were in high demand. All the cul-de-sac middle-class neighborhoods were taken, including mine. My brother and I were assigned to the Litchfield route, which was essentially the low-income housing projects. There was a diverse mix of families, some who spoke English and some who did not. Some were legal citizens and others were not. There were large groups of children who filled up the school buses so the complex had their own bus stops. I remember thinking about how little space they had and how it was shared — from the buildings to their grass to their bedrooms. I was acutely aware that while my family, in the hierarchy of the "haves" and the "have nots" had very little, but I suddenly realized there were people who had even less. It was humbling.

My customers were low-income families, and I was happy to deliver the paper to them. We had to work seven days a week and deliver before 7:00 a.m. on weekends. The Lady would drop us off in her minivan. We would load up our bags with papers, then meet back at the van about halfway, which landed at Dorothy's building. Then, we would meet the minivan at the last section and finish up. While we were delivering, The Lady was labeling the payment envelopes, rolling coins, and making payment notices.

Dorothy was a Caucasian elderly woman who lived alone in one of the first-floor apartments. She always seemed lonely. She kept her white hair in curlers, no matter what time of day it was, but it's not like she was going anywhere. Her right eye was always turned to the side and it appeared as if she was blind in that eye — it was cloudy and weird-looking.

When we approached Dorothy's door, we were given instructions to knock first. "Knock three times so I know it is you. Never leave the paper at the door, it will get stolen," she would say. On the weekends, we knew we were Dorothy's wakeup-call service; she woke up to our knock and she lived for the weekend papers. The Saturday papers were just better than the Monday-through-Fridays, but the Sundays were twice as big and had all the coupons. It would take her at least two minutes to open the door because she had a series of deadbolts stacked up on her doorjamb. It was her version of a wind chime, the metal clicks, drags, and bings played for her, making her feel safe in her own rituals. Believe me, she used her peephole. Even with our three-knock rule, she would still play it safe. Dorothy taught me how consistency and caring for my customers paid me back with purpose. We received small porcelain knick-knacks for Christmas and a steady $2 tip each Sunday in her envelope, which was always collected on time.

After a while we started to see things — drugs deals and fist fights in front of the buildings. We started to smell things too (*OK, now I know what marijuana smells like*). We started to hear things — screaming, fighting, struggle. We started to hear about things, like stabbings, shootings, and gangs. This was our introduction to a whole new world ... a world where our kind of middle-class abuse seemed small.

The buildings were filled with apartments that shared a common stairwell and went up three floors. There was a peculiar smell to each stairwell. In one building, it was as if curry was mixed with rice, beans, and cigarettes. After a while, the smell of the stairs made me so nauseated, so I would hold my breath, just like at home.

We ran up, tossed our papers in front of our customer's doors, then ran back down, grateful to be at the bottom. *Just one more building, just one more paper.* We were paper-delivering machines, and I was developing a work ethic.

We had just finished our Saturday route and come back home. I was counting to 13 as my feet pounded out the familiar blueprint up the stairs. The bathroom door was shut.

"Sissy, are you in there?"

"Yeah."

"Where is Dad?"

"He is sleeping."

"What are you doing in there?"

"I am giving myself a haircut."

SHIT.

"OK, I need you to open the door please."

"I am almost done."

"Please open the door or I will have to knock down the door."

There she was — sitting on the counter, with scissors in her hand, covered in blonde strands of hair that were no longer attached to their follicles. She had nothing left, except a rat tail in the back, but only because she couldn't reach. Her hair was shorter than a #3 buzz cut.

"Oh my god, WHAT did you do?

"I wanted a haircut like Michelle. Michelle's mom gets her haircuts."

I gasped. I think I actually screamed.

"What the hell is going on in this house!"

My sister looked like a boy. There was nothing we could do, other than let her hair grow out. When we were out in public, people would come up to us and ask her how her treatments were going. On a few occasions, some empathetic women would hand us a few dollars. The problem was that this haircut represented a lot more than the fact that my little sister was alone in the bathroom with scissors for several hours. It represented our version of poverty.

With our dad out of work, The Lady explained the repercussions of being on one income and how she would have to work overtime. The Lady never went to college, so working as a correctional officer at the female prison was the best she could do, plus it had state benefits. The mortgage was too expensive. The groceries were too expensive. We would have to buy our own school clothes and if we wanted to keep dancing and playing sports, we would have to contribute our work money to those activities. I knew this was bad. Ever since my parents had filed bankruptcy when I was 4, I knew I didn't want to go through that again. I remembered the sequence of bankruptcy, renting a house, getting robbed, and changing schools.

Hungry and Broke

My sister's ill-fated haircut brought our situation into clear focus for me.
I began having a flashback of the last time we lost everything, and it took
years to start over. It was my first day at Fall Brook Elementary. I was in the
second grade, and I started my own tradition of wearing a dress on every
first day of school. This dress was a collared, sleeveless denim button-down
top with a blue and black flowy floral bottom. I was nervous and shy, but
excited to learn. I was on a roll, reading three books a day — and now
I would have access to a new library. The Lady didn't leave me lunch money,
so I packed my brown bag lunch with a PB&J — creamy, not crunchy, with
grape jelly, sliced diagonally on Wonder Bread. I cannot believe I used to
eat Wonder Bread. The only thing in the fridge to drink was a two-liter of
Pepsi, so I packed a plastic mug with a snap-down straw and poured the
Pepsi inside.

In the cafeteria, they sat us by our classroom. The lunch aides sat two tables
per class, as they called the "lunch money kids" to get in line. I remember
my entire class getting up from the table, with their lunch money in their
hands. I was the only kid left behind.

I looked behind me and all I saw was a sea of faces, with mouths wide open,
laughter echoing, as they pointed, cooed and cawed while my head started
to spin and their faces blurred out into a fuzzy memory, one that has been
stored for over 25 years. There were tables full of kids just laughing at me
because I was alone.

I felt my stomach pulse with nausea and butterflies, which at the time just
felt like an instant burst of the flu. I couldn't throw up on the table and be
the loser who threw up in front of everyone on the first day at a new school,
so I cupped my hands, put them in front of my mouth and #*FNDFK$Q_@#.
I walked over to the lunch lady who was monitoring the exit. I showed her
my hands and she pointed to the nurse's office, where I walked slowly, then
dumped my barf into the school nurse's sink.

In 7th grade, there wasn't bread, peanut butter, or jelly at the house
anymore, so I couldn't pack lunches like I used to. And because I was a kid
with zero financial-planning skills, my paper route money didn't always last
through the week like I had intended it to. I didn't know what budgeting was

and one trip to the mall would leave me with cute matching school outfits, while I was without lunch money. I had to learn how to be resourceful.

I had a friend named Alison who was always hungry with me. She and I teamed up with our begging faces and puppy eyes, as we approached every boy in our class who was approaching puberty and who might have a soft spot for a girl asking for food money. We would ask them each for a quarter every day. These boys were so nice, because they would get annoyed, but they could not say no. We would usually get $1.00 - $1.50 each per day and we would use that at the school store during our recess to get snacks. When the lunch hour came, I would use that time for socializing instead of eating. (Plus, those pre-packaged snacks were much more edible than the school lunches.)

And the Workaholism Begins...

My OCD carried over into the classroom and I needed to have those perfect grades. I had to raise my hand and be well-liked by my teachers. I had to compete in the spelling bees, class plays, and gym-class football games. I wanted to have everything planned, organized, and clean. Sometimes I would re-write my journal over and over again until I felt my handwriting was perfect. I had more torn-out pages than I did entries. I wore perfectly coordinated outfits and had to stop buying white sneakers — because once they got dirty, I would bleach them but I couldn't ever wear them again. I couldn't focus if there was a mess. I couldn't enjoy free time unless my homework was done. I couldn't go on that stage without practicing more than anyone else. I wanted to be good. I wanted to be smart. I wanted to feel safe, but I only felt safe when I was in control. And there were two subjects that made me feel out of control: food and money.

Part 2
90-DEGREE TURN

Even when feeling utterly empty, the glimpses started to appear — the freedom, passions, and my voice audible above the surface, where it had been buried since birth.

The hunger persisted — for an escape, for change, for love, but I could see the opportunities of my future, outside the dark door. I could see how my differences were getting me somewhere, as I stopped listening to the others and started only listening to my own voice.

I deviated from the path I was given, to create my own, as I deflected my emotions and pushed through sadness to find anger, through weakness to find strength, and through fatigue to find energy. I needed my energy to get out of here, and I needed there to be a ready place for when I got out.

Kaleidoscope

A fake image shows on the screen.
It plays all day,
and changes at night.
Like a kaleidoscope —
No color ...
Only black and white.

Light during the day,
and darkness at night,
Going back and forth,
180 degrees each time.
I long to break free.

The caution tape blocks the doorway,
the white noise machine stays on.
No one wears glasses,
but we are all blinded ...
Our eyes and ears just turn off.
Senseless but still alive, I fight to emerge
from the darkness.

I leave. I see.
I hear. I speak.
I find the truth.
(It was hiding
behind every messy corner.)
Because what appears clean on the outside
is messy on the inside.
What looks like suburbia
is sometimes a living hell.

7

Homeless

It was the morning of my sophomore year dance recital — Saturday, May 15, 2004. The noise of my alarm clock sounded, and I felt the butterflies swirling around in my stomach and inside my head. My eyes opened to diffused sunlight shining across my feet underneath the blanket. I was too excited to be hungry. As for work, I had the weekend off so I could perform in the Saturday evening and the Sunday matinee recitals. I got to sleep in, and I felt no stress, just nerves and excitement. Performing on stage was my therapy. I did not have to speak what I was feeling, but my body could move to the music, snatch the energy from the crowd, and use it to power my turns, and arabesques.

> Performing on stage was my therapy. I did not have
> to speak what I was feeling, but my body could move
> to the music, snatch the energy from the crowd,
> and use it to power my turns, and arabesques.

I moved from my bed and sat on my carpet. My feet were touching, knees wide, in butterfly stretch. My hips were tight. I used my elbows to press my knees into the floor and I breathed calmly with my eyes closed. Then I opened my legs into second position, pointed both sets of toes, and reached through the center, then to the right and left. The more I stretched, the more ready I felt to perform on stage. This was just my morning stretch, but I would still go to the high school four hours early to settle in backstage, laying out all my costume changes, touching up my hair and makeup, passing around lip stick, Sour Patch Kids and Cape Cod chips.

I held my stretch while meditating before I realized that the house was suspiciously quiet. OK, not suspicious, just fortuitous. No one was home. *How did I get so lucky?*

I opened my two windows — the air was clean. My room was oozing daylight, tranquility, and safety, as if the four walls were hugging me tight. I lay down, stretching my arms above my head and stretching my pointed toes as far as they could go beyond my ankles, preparing for my pointe shoe arches and pink tight tendus. I visualized myself doing all my dance numbers on stage — tap, jazz, ballet, pointe, lyrical, and character choreography. I would replay these all day, so that my anxiety of blacking out on stage could be put to rest.

Ring, ring!

I answered my cordless phone. "Hello?"

It was The Lady.

"Your father passed away this morning."

There was an awkward pause and I could hear her lightly sobbing.

"OK."

Silence.

"Thank you for letting me know."

"You're welcome."

That was it. A brief conversation from two emotional robots. I was 16 and my dad was dead.

 That was it. A brief conversation from two emotional robots. I was 16 and my dad was dead.

The truth was that he was at peace now, and so was I. I already felt the air shifting. I felt lighter. I felt relieved. It was over now — the hospital equipment lingering around our house, the hospice visits and resentment toward me for not going, the family pressuring me to feel or act a certain way because my dad was dying, the financial stress and all the late payment notices from my dance teacher. I had an abusive alcoholic father who left me with anger, but without love and no protection. His diagnosis with a degenerative disease did not take away what kind of person he was. My empathy for his suffering didn't mean I had forgotten all he had done to us.

Six months earlier, my friend Paul's mom passed away from breast cancer. Her name was Jill and I thought she was an angel on earth. I had known her since kindergarten, where I used to sit with her on the field trip bus rides instead of sitting with my friends. I just loved her. In high school, there would be a group of us hanging out in Paul's basement, playing pool and watching movies. Jill was sick, but she would never miss a trip down those stairs to bring us homemade chocolate chip cookies, Papa Gino's pizza, and fresh lemonade. She was a doting mother to all of us.

When Jill died, I could barely make it through school. I was heartbroken — for Paul, for his family, and for the world, because she was a special mom. I mourned her death as if I was losing my own special mom, because it was the idea of having one and losing her that got me. At her memorial service, I had a complete emotional breakdown. I wasn't used to feeling sadness, so when it came, it all came at once.

Now, my own dad was dead, and it felt a lot different. I stared at myself in the mirror. Why wasn't I crying? *Something must be wrong with me.* I felt a burst of joy. IT'S FINALLY OVER. Six years of ALS, watching death fall upon our dark doorstep. *Something must be wrong with me.*

I only told two of my best friends at my dance recital — Liesl and Courtney. I thought they understood more about the situation than most, but they both loved their fathers and probably internalized how they really felt toward my non-emotional response to my father's death. I could not focus on what everyone else thought anymore; what was more important to me was that they were going to keep this a secret. There was no need to bring uncomfortable attention or emotions into this.

That night, I performed to a faceless audience without family members watching, but I pretended that my dad was there. I pictured him standing in the back, with a voice, telling me he was sorry for everything and that he was proud. I pictured him telling me I was a beautiful dancer, instead of telling me he hated being at these boring dance recitals. I felt the forgiveness radiate from the back of the auditorium to my pointed toes on the stage. I was processing — my body flowing in the form of soft brush strokes across the stage, releasing me toward a new kind of emotional freedom. I felt more connected to the music and movement than ever before.

That night, I performed to a faceless audience without family members watching, but I pretended that my dad was there. I pictured him standing in the back, with a voice, telling me he was sorry for everything and that he was proud.

We were on this innocent teenage high as we left the recital and met at our favorite restaurant, Friendly's. It was easy to forget about what was happening at home. We were eating our Monster Mashes sprinkled in M&M's and topped with whipped cream and extra cherries. Our loud chatter filled the restaurant as we reflected on our stressful "quick changes" backstage, how the music was too quiet during tap, and how so-and-so's pointe shoe fell off. Then Molly started asking around the table, "Who came to the recital to watch you tonight?"

I stayed quiet, not answering. Everyone else chimed in and she noticed I was the only dancer without a response.

"Danielle, did your dad come tonight?"

She remembered my dad being the "nice parent" from long-ago second-grade sleepovers.

"No, he is in a wheelchair. You know, in his hospice place."

"Oh, I didn't know. I am sorry. Can he still come in his wheelchair?"

"No."

"I am sorry. Well, did your mom come?"

"No. No one came. Because my dad ... he, he died this morning."

Molly ran into the bathroom crying. I jumped up to follow her, suddenly consoling my classmate over my dad's death. I promised her it was OK and explained that I was trying to keep it a secret, but I didn't want to lie.

Mourning

I stayed numb, moving through the motions of the funeral services, school, and work. The Lady notified the guidance counselor, and he notified my teachers. I was called over the intercom to go see him. I knocked on his door, he asked me to sit down, and he started pushing me to talk about what happened. I sat there, straight-faced and on mute. I had nothing to say. I was stubborn and he sent me out, slamming the door behind me.

My gym teacher gave me a Charms Blow Pop. My English teacher gave me a D on a project that was due the day of the wake. (I had forgotten the written portion of my project at home. I told her it was completed, but that I had a lot going on at home and I must have forgotten it on my desk.) *No exceptions.* The D was mine to keep.

As I adjusted to the "new normal" of life without a father, I only told a handful of friends and they were sworn to secrecy. Everyone else found out from their parents reading the obituaries in the *Sentinel & Enterprise*. My dance teacher and previous teachers surprised me by showing up to the wake. I guess somehow it got through the grapevine, to some extent.

My brother had a crowd at our father's wake — his classmates, baseball team, former coaches, football players, and basketball players. One of his female classmates returned to school the next day, sharing the story of how she couldn't believe I wasn't crying at my dad's wake. The rumor got back to me — "Danielle is a heartless bitch. Can you believe she didn't cry at her own dad's wake?" I was so angry I was seeing red. I kept thinking, *"You don't know me!"* I wanted to see her in school so bad — wanted to confront her. But after not seeing her in the crowded school hallways for a few days, I messaged her on AIM. I sent paragraphs, letting her know that she was the worst person in our high school for passing judgment like this on someone she did not know. She needed to mind her own business, because she had no idea what kind of person my dad was. "Besides, no one in this family cries."

Seized by Stoicism

It was not a normal grieving experience. I had already lost my dad years ago. No one would understand how I felt. I assumed I was just a cold-hearted bitch, after all. Instead of honoring my emotions and knowing that I was a good person (even if I didn't cry when my dad died), it was easier to hide in denial, so I hid my emotions and I hid them well.

I was busy in those months following the loss of my dad. A new school year started — I was playing tennis almost every day after school, I had dance three nights a week, and I was working 40-hour weeks as a Subway sandwich artist, which mostly consisted of weekend doubles and missing Friday-night football games. I preferred to stay busy, and I was an obvious over-achiever. I was the secretary of our class government, I planned our Junior Prom, and I had a schedule full of all honors classes. My load was heavy, but I loved to push my own limits and see just how much I could do, while giving 100% to it all. Plus, being busy meant fewer hours at home, and more work hours meant that affording college became more possible. I had begun to see college as my one-way ticket out.

There is no doubt that my busy schedule led to a lack of sleep. Most days, I ran off adrenaline, but when the classes extended to 90 minutes, there was a strong chance they would put me right to sleep. My anatomy teacher started one class by stating how he could not believe the student who slept on her desk in his class every day had the highest grade. I needed the class time for sleep, but I would use any spare minute to study and do home-work, which included the bus rides to tennis matches, slow time at work on Sundays, and midnight hours. I had to have straight A's, I had to hit my 40 hours at work, and I had to excel in every commitment I made. Until it all started exploding.

I always closed the restaurant on the weekends. I left Subway around 11:30 p.m. and then went straight to bed.

The shaking woke me up. My body was shaking. I couldn't stop it.
I couldn't open my eyes, but I kept trying, as I felt warm urine run down my legs and soak into my sheets.

I stayed still, making sure it was over. *Holy shit. I had just had a seizure.*

I got up, gathered my blankets and sheets, and walked downstairs to the washing machine. The Lady was sleeping on the brown sofa, which she had moved into the pool room to replace the recliner. I heard her from where she was.

"What are you doing?"

"I just had a seizure and I wet the bed."

"A seizure?"

"Yeah. I woke up to my body shaking and then I wet the bed."

"OK. I don't know why you would be having a seizure."

"I think I need to go see a doctor."

"You may need to see Dad's neurologist."

For the next few days, I was thunderstruck by fear. I did not want it to happen again and I was afraid of becoming epileptic. *What was wrong with me?*

The following Saturday, I drove my two friends in my "teal mobile" to Solomon Pond Mall, which was a half hour away via the highway. The teal mobile was my first car and it cost $800. Gas was $1.87 per gallon and my insurance was over $200 a month, because I was a young female driver on my own insurance policy. The car was a Dodge Shadow — I think they may have only made a few hundred of them. The exterior was half teal, half rust. The roof leaked above the driver's seat and every time it rained or snowed, I would go to school with wet pants. That whole "It looks like I peed my pants" thing was less funny after the seizure incident. I had a pink fuzzy steering wheel cover and a trash can in the back for any trash (with thanks to my OCD). It was an unattractive vehicle, but it was mine and it took me places, like the mall.

On our way home, we were on a highway where the speed limit was 65 mph. I started feeling funny. I couldn't breathe and I missed our exit.

We looped around on the highway again, but my chest was pounding, and I was hyperventilating when my feet went numb.

"Umm, Danielle, you are going 90 miles an hour."

"I can't feel my feet!!! I can't see!!! What is happening?"

"Oh my god. OK, pull over at this next exit and I will drive."

I missed the next three exits.

"Danielle, it is OK. Breathe. We are going 100 now, so try to stay calm so we can pull over."

"I can't feel my legs, I can't feel anything!!"

After circling past our exit four times, I was able to drive us back to Leominster safely. My friends were scared we were going to crash. I was afraid I was going to die. I didn't understand what was happening with my body.

 My friends were scared we were going to crash. I was afraid I was going to die.

The next week, I printed out my MapQuest directions and unsafely drove with them on my steering wheel on that same highway, to a town further away than the mall. This was before cell phones and GPS. The doctor seemed concerned about my seizure and ordered an EKG and an MRI. He told me until I was cleared, he didn't want me driving.

WOAHHHH, BUDDY.

"I need my license. I need to drive. I go to school, and I have a job. And dance. And tennis. And I NEED to drive."

He didn't understand what this license meant to me. He didn't understand that I *needed* to get out of that house and that I *needed* to work. It was my salvation.

He called The Lady promptly after I left his office. When I returned from my appointment, she wanted me to give up my license. I told her there was no way in hell I was going to give up driving unless the doctor had medical proof that the seizures might keep coming. The Lady didn't care about my seizure, but she *did* want to gain some control back. If I couldn't drive, it would be like freshman year all over again. She started by taking away my telephone, then my TV, and I'd end up being grounded for an entire year.

The yelling went back and forth, gaining volume, until we settled on the fact that both of us should burn in hell. At least that held her over until the test results came back.

 The yelling went back and forth, gaining volume, until we settled on the fact that both of us should burn in hell.

I was cleared neurologically.

"Danielle, you are experiencing severe anxiety attacks."

Everything went fuzzy after that.

"Can I keep my license?"

"Yes, but if this happens again while you are driving, you shouldn't be driving, and you need to go see a psychiatrist."

I wasn't going to see anyone, but I agreed to what he said and got the hell out of there.

Without parents who were nurturing and kind, and because no one else really knew what was going on in my life, I carried on with the mania of working too much, studying too much, socializing too much, sleeping too little, and never once taking time to care for my body or my mind. Intellectually, I knew that my chaotic life and dysfunctional family were making me sick —but I was just a kid who was doing the very best with what few tools she had. Distraction and escape were how I survived. My body was trying to send me a critical message, but I didn't know how to listen. I just kept going, doing what I knew how to do: survive.

That year, history class was first period. One day, immediately after my anxiety attacks reared their ugly head, we had a quiz and Mr. Robichaud gave us 10 minutes to study before he handed it out. I was quizzing Jeff and Ross at my table when I started to feel funny again. I stood up to rush to the bathroom and I fell straight down on the floor. I couldn't breathe. I couldn't see and I couldn't feel my legs. The whole class saw me, and I started spiraling into a fit of hyperventilation, which was triggered even more from embarrassment. Jeff took my arms and Ross grabbed my feet, and they held my body just above the floor as they carried me down to the nurse's office. I don't remember what the teacher did, but my classmates were certainly good under pressure.

The nurse called my house and The Lady never picked up. No big surprise. To my knowledge, she slept through every call for every year I was in school (and the calls weren't frequent — a call from the school should have been cause for alarm and attention, but it never was). The nurse gave up and she sent me home.

This continued to happen during school and during work. When it happened at school, I was sent to the nurse again.

"Didn't your dad just die?"

"That was six months ago. Actually, six months ago today."

"Well, do you know what anxiety is?"

"Not really."

"Anxiety is when trauma is suppressed in your subconscious. You may need to talk to someone. It is possible that your father's death is causing these anxiety attacks."

"No, it's not that. I'm fine. I'm just tired. I work a lot."

Everything is FINE. *FINE, FINE, FINE.* God, I was so stubborn. And in denial.

Grand Theft Auto

I kept working and moving forward; it was all I knew how to do. I saved up my minimum-wage paychecks and upgraded my vehicle from my $800 side-of-the-road find, the Dodge Shadow "teal mobile," to a $2,400 Plymouth Neon that I found on Craigslist. Unable to afford vehicles from car dealerships, I had to be resourceful to find these deals, and I paid for both vehicles in cash. I remember that handing over that $2,400 felt like I was paying $20,000. Paying for anything that large was emotional because I was working so hard ... and now my bank account was empty again. When it came to money, I felt like I was always at zero because I was paying for absolutely everything I needed to live, with the exception of the roof currently over my head. Ultimately, I was paying for my independence and, as hard as it was, I was willing to keep working and paying.

One hot summer night, I felt an extreme sense of anxiety, like a caged animal try to shout, "GET ME OUT OF HERE!!!"

An odd, suspicious silence lingered in the house. The silence made me want to flee as badly as I wanted to escape on the nights filled with screaming. That night, The Lady went to work, my sister was asleep, my brother was in his basement cavern, and I didn't want to be home. I called my friend Paul and he said he could pick me up in his dad's convertible.

After driving around, gossiping, and killing time, I knew I needed to call it a night. It was almost 1:00 a.m., so I asked Paul to take me back home. I was falling asleep, my head resting against the inside of the car door, the breeze pushing and pulling the wispy flyaway hairs around my face onto my forehead. The air was cool and the sky was dark but lit with light pollution from the streetlights, house lights, and our headlights. I felt the rhythm of Birchcroft Road beneath our rolling tires and I opened my eyes right before the sweeping corner that led to my house.

As we pulled in front of the house in Paul's dad's car, *my* car slowly left the driveway and started down the road. Half asleep, I stuttered the words, unsure if I was seeing things, "That's weird. I swear my car just drove by us."

I had to wake myself up to let it sink in that my gold Plymouth Neon was not parked in my driveway where I left it.

"Oh my god!! Someone stole my car!!!"

"Should we call the police??"

"No, follow my car!"

We spun around like a horseshoe, sped down the street, and approached the slow-moving vehicle, with a suspicious driver who wasn't driving straight or fast.

"I am so scared!!! Oh my god, who the hell stole my car?!"

We pulled up toward the driver's side and the driver rolled down the window. *It was my brother.*

I cannot explain how the constellation of feelings washed over me — the shock, anger, and a feeling of having had my personal property and space violated or invaded. My brother couldn't talk. He was drunk. That is why he was driving so slowly. He was drunk and he stole my car, but I had my keys on me and I had just one spare key that was well hidden — inside a little box that was inside my jewelry box, under a stack of folded clothes, inside my closet. It would have taken hours to find, after going through my entire room, looking inside every door and drawer. My only safe space had been invaded. I couldn't breathe, just like the night The Lady came in my room blowing cigarette smoke everywhere, including in my face. Just like the night we had the robbers sifting through our house while we were asleep, with the rare chance of our front door being left open after Brianna went home. I hated this place and everyone in it.

Nomad

As the summer dragged on, life continued pretty much as it always had. I did my level best to stay away from my siblings and my mom, to hide out when I absolutely had to be in the house, and to be a star student, star dancer, star employee. Escapism was what kept me from the edge of despair, though it also took me dangerous close to collapse. I pushed forward, flirting with adulthood, believing I would eclipse this difficult life someday in the fore-seeable future.

I now had money in my bank account and time to go to the beach with friends. My friend Val and I started a car washing business for our friends. While The Lady was sleeping, we would use the hose in my driveway. Entrepreneurial at heart (but not really knowing it), I always had a project and a way to make money while serving others. We made a CD of our favorite summer songs and we played them on repeat while we washed our friends' cars for tips only (because we found it fun). During the summer nights, we would always make 11:11 wishes* after several Dollar Menu stops. Our favorite summer activity was piling four of us in the front seat of a Ford F150 and going through the McDonald's drive-through window. We would order unhealthy quantities of chicken nuggets and extra pickles, hoping the window workers would give us some sort of reaction. We could never keep straight faces. We found way more amusement in ourselves than they found in us. In those moments, life was simple and joyful and carefree.

I wanted that feeling to last for 24 entire hours. Maybe longer — days, weeks, months. So I grabbed a trash bag of clothes and shoes. I took my 13 steps down and into the kitchen. It was around dinner time, so The Lady had awoken.

I looked at her straight in the eye.

"I am moving out. If you try to call the cops or declare me as a runaway again, you will never see me for as long as I live. I can't be here anymore. I am moving in with Val for the summer."

She was shocked. She had a boyfriend now and she was more distracted and less defiant.

"OK."

I played some reverse psychology on her (knowing she lived to control me) and I got her right where I wanted her, at my mercy. Maybe she was thinking I'd be back after the summer — that I would still be her at-home daughter and the object of her vitriol and cruelty. She didn't know then that I was

---

* 11:11 was our lucky number — whether morning or night, it was our lucky time to make a wish on the car clock. I remember the car clock being our most likely place to mark the passage of time — because that's where we mostly were, in the car on summer nights, looking for a place to go. We found laughter and the cure of boredom right there in the confines of the car; it was where we had our freedom.

planning to go to college and never come back. I was determined that once I left for school, she would NEVER see me again. But that was my little secret for now.

I had just one more year of high school to survive. That entire summer before my senior year, I shared a full bed with my friend Val. Her family was generous enough to have me (for which I was incredibly grateful) so I tried to stay out of the way — leaving early in the morning and coming home late at night. I was homeless. I just needed a bed and a shower. I didn't eat out of their fridge and I didn't open their windows. I was like a ghost in the night, and I was comfortable being invisible.

I was homeless. I just needed a bed and a shower. I didn't eat out of their fridge and I didn't open their windows. I was like a ghost in the night, and I was comfortable being invisible.

We had a fun summer, full of chicken nuggets and car washes. We were innocent. The most scandalous thing I was doing was wearing tube tops — with my first strapless bra (although I really didn't need one). We were working hard and laughing harder. We were independent. We would drive an hour to the beach at 10:00 p.m., just to put our feet in the water and drive right back.

I was with my friends every day or night, depending on my work schedule. I went to my cousin Kim's house for more *Trading Spaces* marathons. Some of the episodes started to repeat at this point, but Vern Yip's words echoed in my head: There is a difference between a house and a home. *A house is a structure that provides a roof over your head. A home is a place where you love to be.*

I was homeLESS.

Before I knew it, it was time to start making my escape plan. My college acceptance letter came in (letter … singular). I applied to just one school — Endicott College — and it was a miracle I got in. Every college application cost $50 - $100 at that time and I was gambling. My transcript was strong, but the interior design program required an art portfolio. I wasn't good at

art. I made a few construction paper and watercolor straw-blowing pieces*
and went to my high school art teacher's house for him to scan them in,
making them look more presentable than hard copies. This was a wealthy
college, and if they knew I came from a single-parent home or saw The
Lady's tax returns, I fear they would not have accepted me.

I applied early, so my letter came in early. The dorm room deposit was $500
and, even with a scholarship of almost 50%, I would still owe more than
$20,000 a year. I went from screaming in excitement to crying. I called my
friend in agonizing tears, "How was I going to make this work?"

I was back to sleeping at my house again and the stress was ever-present.
College was my way out of here. I had so much pressure to make this work,
but there were no guarantees.

I left the FAFSA financial aid paperwork on the stove with note that read:
"Can you please fill this out?"

I came home the next day to check the stove. The paperwork was still there.
The note was still there. I walked into the pool room, where The Lady was
sitting on her brown sofa.

"Can you please fill this out?"

"Why would I do that for *you*?"

---

* A type of art where paint is blown through a straw to make an abstract design with the
drip marks

Finish line

Oh, she was a runaway, always good at running away.
She ran at night and during the day.
Suitcase packed for hopeful overnight stays,
hoping friends would keep her that way.

Yes, she was a runaway.
A fast runner and always afraid.
Up the stairs or down the street
were her fastest times to beat.
She locked the bathroom door for safety
'til he learned to pick the lock,
So he threw her down the stairs ..
for another concussion
and more nightmares.

She never reached the finish line, zero to eighteen,
letting go of foster care as her biggest dream.
She lived in a state of imprisonment,
impatiently waiting to be set free.
Freedom was what she fought for,
but the nightmares never stopped ...
Visions of running, and never making it out.

Because she was never fast enough.

The Girl Who Disappeared

High school graduation was like a funeral for me. A farewell tour. A breakup.

I had plans to attend college in fall and to never return to 99 Birchcroft Road or to Leominster, Massachusetts. I couldn't tell anyone my plans, because I had too many goodbyes to deliver and I simply couldn't handle some of them. Without my friends, their families, my classmates, dance class, tennis team, student government, and co-workers, I wouldn't have made it. How could I ever say goodbye to them all?

Senior year was a great year, and possibly the only year I would have been OK with slowing down. There is something about when you have the last of something (the last morsel of cake, the last kiss, the last pep rally, the last recital), you want it to linger forever. Outside of the house, I was surrounded by so much love. I was sad to leave the classrooms filled with my friends. I was sad to leave my boyfriend, Anthony, who went from being with me in the front seat of the McDonald's drive-through to being my first serious relationship. I was sad to leave my tennis partner, Nicole, who became like a sister to me. I was sad to leave my dance studio and Miss Heidi, my dance teacher of 15 years, and accept that my days performing on a stage and telling my story through my movement were probably ending. The summer night drives, and late-night grocery store stops for gallons of ice cream were going to end. The prom planning, birthday-party planning, and beach-day planning were over. I had been waiting my whole life to leave this house and this town, but I never wanted to leave the people. That was just the unfortunate part of the deal.

 Outside of the house, I was surrounded by so much love.
... I had been waiting my whole life to leave this house
and this town, but I never wanted to leave the people.

New Faces, New Frustrations

The Lady was dating a co-worker from the prison, which was weird for so many reasons. I only saw John a few times when I was grabbing a new weeks' worth of clothes in between sleepovers with my friends, but he was handsome, polite, and normal. I had never seen The Lady hug, kiss, hold hands, or show any romantic feelings toward my dad — but for her boyfriend, she had googly eyes. It was uncomfortable to witness any love coming out of this monster, but the hardest part for me to understand was how he didn't see her for who she really was. Didn't he think it was weird that her children wanted nothing to do with her?

John had a daughter a few years older than my sister. They seemed to get along, which worked out because The Lady would take my sister to John's house almost every weekend — in a town that was an hour away from Leominster. I was no longer my little sister's underage guardian. An empty house on the weekends seemed like a paradise to a rebellious teenager. One Saturday night I came home close to midnight, after closing the sandwich shop. There were cars lining the streets and I could barely get in my front door. There were at least 100 high schoolers in my house, with a puddle of beer on the kitchen floor. I wove through the crowd, asking for my brother. He was in the basement with his new girlfriend, who was in my grade and in my classes. *Oh, this is happening.* I told him this needed to end, immediately. I spent an hour clearing everyone out and then several hours cleaning. I cared more about being able to go to bed than I did him getting in trouble the next day — when I would disappear for the week and The Lady would come home. I couldn't sleep with this mess, so I scrubbed, mopped, vacuumed, and sprayed while he and his girlfriend loudly flirted in the basement. As awkward as this was, and as angry as I was, my brother's girlfriend kept him distracted, and that was exactly what I needed. Cleaning up other people's messes was what I had been groomed to do. In a way, I think the cleaning before bed gave me permission to rest and allowed for better sleep with fewer nightmares.

I woke up to the early summer sun. I was dressed in a loose t-shirt, no bra, and underwear. I folded my leg outside of the comforter and then jumped with a silent scream. There was an unidentified teenage boy sleeping on my carpet, in my bedroom, on my floor, bedside. I had just inadvertently touched him with my toes. I stared, trying to recognize him, and trying to remember whether I had heard something (*anything*) in the middle of the night. There is one advantage to getting a few hours of sleep — it is usually a deep sleep. I tiptoed to my dresser, grabbed a pair of pants, and snuck out of my room. I made a quick detour into the bathroom and then out of my house, where I could try to remain calm even though my thoughts were reeling. *ARE YOU FUCKING KIDDING ME?*

I never tattled on my brother — for the party, the beer, or the dude sleeping in my room — because there was no benefit in that. Keeping quiet, on the other hand, might make it seem like I did him a favor ... and I could use that kind of credit in the bank. Now I might have something on my side to keep him less focused on hurting me. I made it clear to him that if anything ever happened to me from his creepy friends, then I would be sure to get all of them arrested. The Lady would have never found out about the party had she not found a single beer can in the freezer. He was never grounded though; he was still the golden child.

Big Dreams, Big Debts

My friend Liesl's dad agreed to co-sign my student loans so I was able to attend college. Even now, writing those words still seems surreal. I was 18 years old and unable to offer him any collateral, coming from a family who could never and would never pay him back if I didn't do so myself. Still he put his credit on the line to allow me to receive an education — all while he had four children of his own. He knew I was a responsible kid and maybe he knew I needed just one adult to give me a fighting chance. I am so grateful that he had the courage and generosity to be that adult. He was willing to do something that my own birth mother was not willing to do. I promised him I would never miss a payment. I could not believe how lucky I was.

Looking back on the day I got the nerve to ask for his help, I recall it as one of the most humbling questions I ever had to ask. I didn't like owing anyone anything. I was fiercely independent and, truth be told, I didn't want to need something this *big* from any adult. I had no choice. Education was my ticket to becoming someone and it was my only ticket out.

In my family, we weren't big on college ... or on education in general. No one ever looked at my report cards and no one asked if homework was done or how school was going. My dad's focus was on my brother's sports, but ironically, it was me — the child — who was always trying to get my parents to show an interest in my academic pursuits. I would show my dad my report cards and tell him he had to pay me $20 if I made straight A's. I would wave my report card in his face, and he would slip the twenty out from his wallet, with very little commentary, and hand it over. Two of my uncles had owned gas stations and they were the most successful people I knew in the family. (But being entrepreneurial was a concept I wouldn't grasp for several more years.) The Lady and my godmother were both correctional officers because, in their words, they "didn't have a college education." And my dad sort of stumbled into the industry by happenstance. College was something I wanted so badly, for so many reasons — not the least of which was because it made me even more different from them. *"I'm not like them,"* I knew and wanted to keep believing.

As I sat at my high school graduation ceremony, I felt overwhelmed with emotion. I felt the wound-up energy of the 400+ students behind me. I heard the voices of my friends, in harmony with mine. I saw my boyfriend's parents smiling at me from the auditorium chairs. By virtue of being a senior class officer, I sat in the front row and I could see everyone in the audience (and they could see me). I preferred the lights shade their faces like my dance recitals (it made me feel less self-conscious), but I got up and sang the National Anthem with three friends. Then a larger group of us sang the class graduation song, "In My Life," by the Beatles. Congratulations and goodbye to the Class of 2006, because in 12 weeks, my dreams were coming true.

Goodbye and Good Luck

Following graduation, our high school had a tradition of "beach week" — where everyone rented houses and spent a week drinking too much in Hampton Beach, New Hampshire, about an hour away from our hometown. I was focused on saving up as much money as possible (seeing as college was already $80,000 at face value, without including interest) so I opted out. Also, because my family was full of alcoholics and addicts, I decided in high school that I was not going to drink alcohol. It was too big of a risk for me, and I didn't need it. I was happy without it. The problem was that (to every-one else) it was an oddity; I am sure it made me less cool and I felt I didn't fit it at parties. I was always the designated driver, which made me realize how much I hated being the *only one* and I hated being noticed for being *the only one*. I preferred to just exist ... I wanted to be part of the crowd.

I visited beach week during its first night — after my shift at work and revealing my new, dramatic haircut. I had grown out my hair over the past four years and the day after high school graduation, I cut off 12 inches and sent it to the charity, Locks of Love. It was a dream of mine to do this, which I timed out perfectly (they say a drastic change of hair style was the best remedy for a breakup). My breakup was a big one — not with my boyfriend, but an entire community, and a collection of friends I adored. It occurred to me that this was also the kind of breakup where one person loved the other more than they were loved back. I was the one who loved everyone a little more (because, to me, they were all more than friends ... they were family).

The last summer before college was a blast. I had graduation parties nearly every weekend and I saw my friends every hour that I was not at work or sleeping. I was working two full-time jobs: as an assistant teacher at Piccolo Mondo Learning Center during the day Monday through Friday, and as a cashier at CVS with two of my best friends at night and during the week-ends. I worked 80 hours each week and slept in my car or on the breakroom table during my half-hour breaks.

To say that I "threw myself into my work" would be an understatement. I was laser-focused on saving money for college. Plus, the busier I was, the less time I had to think or feel. I associated the feeling of fatigue with successful hard work, which seemed like a healthy decision at the time ... until it became a dangerous pattern.

 The busier I was, the less time I had to think or feel.

With my busy work schedule, sometimes I would stay at my house on weekend nights when I could successfully dodge seeing The Lady and capture a few hours of sleep. As much as I hated that house, I still loved my room, and reality was sinking in. I'd only sleep there a few more times before I left and never saw my room again. I would drive past the house slowly on Saturday nights to determine whether I could sleep there or not — making sure The Lady and my sister were at John's and that my brother was with his girlfriend. There was always a fondness to my bedroom, but now that I knew I would never come back to its yellow walls, two windows, and clean carpet (which gave me safety and peace), I somehow felt better — perhaps nostalgic — about sleeping there from time to time.

One night that summer, I got off work after 9:00 p.m. and did a drive-by at 99 Birchcroft, as if I was an intruder who was casing the joint. There were no cars in the driveway and the lights were off; I was good to go. I parked on the street, entered the house, opened all the windows, sprayed Lysol, and lit all the candles. It was the perfect time to vacuum!

I was 18 now, so I had my own cell phone plan. My flip phone was ringing, but I placed my phone down on the bench instead of answering it. My guy friends were calling me, but I was focused on vacuuming. I was choosing housekeeping over friends tonight. Or so I thought.

Minutes later, I heard a knock on the door.

"Boisse! Boisse! [Pronounced like the capital city of Idaho.] Come hang out!"

SHIT. I panicked and quietly locked the door. I couldn't let my friends see my house like this. It smelled like smoke, there were crumbs and fuzz on the carpets, and there was clutter everywhere.

I continued to vacuum, pretending that I didn't hear the teenagers on the front porch but knowing that they wouldn't leave …so I had to clean as fast as I could.

"Boisse! We know you're in there. Open the door! We aren't leaving until you let us in!"

I sped around with the vacuum cleaner, grabbed countless items that were strewn on the floor and tables, and threw everything inside the coat closet. I ran up and down the stairs with the can of Lysol. I was so embarrassed that I "came from" a family of smokers and clutterers, and I didn't want anyone to walk in and acknowledge this embarrassing discovery. I was good at hiding details about where I came from, and I didn't want to blow it now.

Several minutes passed and the guys were still outside my door, waiting for me to let them in. I unlocked the door, mixing apologizes with exaggerations. (*I needed to shower and no one could smell me like that. I had to finish vacuuming because this was my only time to vacuum when no one was home.*) It was obvious I was uncomfortable, especially when they commented on the fact that they had never been in my house before. I always had excuses and, at the time, those excuses were much easier than the truth.

We always went over to everyone else's houses, so I was not emotionally ready for anyone to just show up at mine. It was like the night of senior prom — a story that warrants telling now.

Just weeks before my high school graduation was my senior prom, a long-awaited event but one that came with a series of stressors. You see, my final hometown dance recital and my senior prom had been scheduled for the same day. After my afternoon recital, I was on a mad dash to get my hair and makeup done before coming back to the neighborhood to meet my prom date, Scott. He made it to my house to pick me up before I arrived. I assumed that

Last dance recital at Miss Heidi's School of Dance, dressed as my senior-year character, Bo Peep from "A Toy Story"

if he didn't see me standing on the front porch, he would wait for me in his car. But he was polite and chivalrous and unaware of my assumptions. Like all good prom dates in American suburbia, he knocked on the front door. Shortly thereafter, he called me on my cell phone, saying he was inside my house, that my mom told him she didn't know where I was, and that she didn't even know I had a dance that evening. My heart sank and my lungs filled with anxiety. *Why did the bitch even let him in?*

I frantically asked, "What do you mean you're in my house? Oh my god, Scott, please get out of there. You can't be in there. You can't talk to my mom. I'm sorry, but can you please get out of there and sit in your car? I will explain later."

As I pulled up to the curb in front of my house a few minutes later, Scott was straight-faced in his car, wondering what the hell was going on. I could see The Lady watching me from inside of the glass door, seeing me in my prom dress — a sight I never wanted her to enjoy. I gave Scott a hug and apologized and explained that "wait for me" meant to wait inside your car. Scott came from a good family and he lived high up on the hill in a large, beautiful home, overlooking the town of Leominster. He was accepted to Harvard University. Now, I worried that he was having second thoughts about me as his prom date, with a dirty house and an uneducated family. No doubt he was wondering why The Lady who gave birth to me didn't even know I had my senior prom that night.

As he got out of his car to put a flower corsage on my wrist, he told me I looked beautiful and gave me a hug. As much as I appreciated those gestures, I just wanted to get in the car and flee. He didn't understand how rushed I was to sneak out of there as quickly as possible.

"Scott, she isn't a good person," I explained. "I can't tell you all the details right now, but I don't let people in my house unless she isn't home. And

*Senior Prom 2006 with
prom date, Scott*

I don't like her meeting my friends. I am just so embarrassed right now. We need to leave before she comes out here."

Just then, I heard the door shut. I looked up above the car to see The Lady walking outside as she awkwardly interjected, "Can I take your picture? I didn't know you had prom tonight."

"Sorry, no. We're late to go take pictures. We have to go." And I slid into the car.

After that, the whole night felt off-kilter, even when Scott and I were dancing after being voted in for Prom Court winners. I could not quite shake that feeling in my stomach. I could possibly get over Scott being in the house and seeing who my mother was, but I could not get over that she saw me in my prom dress. She wasn't supposed to see me. I felt like my special and private moment was invaded. She didn't deserve to see me in my prom dress.

Prom dresses were so expensive and because I couldn't justify spending my college money on a dress for one night, I borrowed my cousin Kim's prom dress. It was "baby yellow" — our favorite color and the color of the walls in my room. It had a strapless, corset top with rhinestone details and a puffy ballroom bottom made of the same sheer material from a ballerina's tutu, but longer and with more layers. The Lady didn't offer to help me pay for a prom dress and she never asked me about my prom so, in my eyes, she stole my moment away, a moment I created for myself. I wanted this memory to be protected from anyone in my crazy family yet, at the last moment, she violated my self-imposed secretive, protective order.

One Last Look

When the fall arrived and it was time to leave for college, I knew that everything was about to be different. I was leaving 99 Birchcroft Road and moving to the campus of Endicott College, in a coastal Massachusetts city an hour away. I was about to become an interior design student, a free agent, a student loan debtor, and a spinner of dreams. The air felt thick and heavy. I was shaky and my face was pale. I knew that my day had come — that day I had been waiting for. I had my car packed. I didn't tell my brother and sister I wasn't coming back here, but each time I carried out a box, I would stare at the house, knowing it was the last time.

 I was leaving 99 Birchcroft Road and moving to the campus of Endicott College, in a coastal Massachusetts city an hour away. I was about to become an interior design student, a free agent, a student loan debtor, and a spinner of dreams.

I only took what I needed — my clothes, shoes, and a plastic bin with sentimental items, such as photo albums, yearbooks, and my first teddy bear. I left my old dance costumes, furniture, jewelry box, knick-knacks, and Beanie Babies behind. By emptying my room completely, I would have made it too obvious that I was never coming back. Plus, realistically, I could only fit so much into my 1995 Plymouth Neon.

I said goodbye to my brother and sister, but I couldn't say goodbye to The Lady. It felt so awkward. I never felt like she was my mother, so what I was feeling wasn't the usual mix of emotions one would expect when leaving to college. I tried to keep it casual while keeping my secret — I was never coming back. If it all worked out the way I imagined, this would be the last time she saw the face of her oldest daughter.

I knew in my heart that once I left, I couldn't come back. It wouldn't be safe, and it wouldn't be healthy for me. There were too many bad memories and I was ready to go somewhere where no one knew me or my family. I needed to disappear, and I hoped that everyone would forget I existed. I had been preparing all summer, spending time with each of my friends, giving them extra-long goodbye hugs, saying that I would miss them and writing them all notes about our favorite memories ... and always signing *Love you!* at the end with xoxoxoxo Dani/Danielle/Boisse, depending on who the note was for.

I drove away that day with my car packed, leaving behind my old dance costumes in my dresser drawers, leaving the bed made, leaving my desk filled with my notebooks inside it. I wasn't coming back, but I did a great job making it look like I was.

College Days

My first year at Endicott was amazing and difficult. I finally had so many things I had longed for. I loved where I lived, I had an ocean view from my dorm window, I had plenty of friends, and I was on the dance team. I was receiving a top-of-the-line private education, I was guaranteed at least three meals a day, and I had my first salad from the cafeteria salad bar. It was all new and it was phenomenal. At the same time, it was hard to relate to all these people who came from money. Their parents would send huge care packages of toilet paper, paper towels, cases of water, and all their favorite snacks. Their laundry cards had $1,000 on them. They drove brand new cars like Hummers, BMWs, and Denalis. As freshman, I learned that the "drinking days" were Thursday through Sunday, so I felt like a loner during beer pong and pre-game activities. Everyone seemed to talk to their moms multiple times a day, because their mom was their best friend. Even I could acknowledge that it was cute, but there was no one like me. The bursar told me she never had "a case like mine" when she asked me to write a letter explaining that I was financially emancipated from my family — because she couldn't finalize my tuition without having a legal guardian fill out my FAFSA application. I wrote a letter stating that my birth mother had not financially supported me in several years, did not act as my legal and caring guardian, and refused to claim me on my student loans. Luckily, this got the deal done. But there's nothing like having to explain your family dysfunction on your way through the door of a wealthy institution when this information quickly blew my cover and revealed that I did not belong there.

While away at college, I became closer with my sister. She was a teenager now, an admittedly immature and annoying teenager. But because I was no longer having to dress her, do her laundry, clean her room, and take her around with me, I seemed to like her more. With the loss of responsibility for her, there was space for some affection. I was also mature enough now to realize that she would always be annoying but that, without me in the house, she was now at serious risk. I wanted to keep tabs on her.

When my fears started to resurface as reality, I checked in with my sister several times a day. The stories weren't promising. My brother's girlfriend had gone away to college and, as a senior in high school, he now had more time for trouble. John had ended the relationship with The Lady and, according to my sister, he told her that he understood who she really was after all. He understood why I wanted nothing to do with her. I felt vindicated and I was happy for John, but I knew what this meant for my sister. She was now home with two experienced abusers who had time on their hands. At first, she would tell me stories like the time my brother beat her in the front yard and then the neighbor across the street beat the shit out of him. Then there was the time my sister had a friend over — that friend ultimately witnessing The Lady abusing my sister, throwing her up against the door, using her body to knock the door from its hinges. The friend went home and told her mom, which meant one less friend for my sister. On the positive side, there was now another witness — a non-family, unbiased witness. How much longer could the community look the other way?

I will never forget the calls I got that first year I was away at college. As my sister told it, she was looking for something in the garage. There were rows of enclosed shelving units on the back wall and as she opened the doors, she found empty boxes of penis enhancers and Asian pornography DVDs. She was mortified, and so was I.

Then came another call — she was hysterical.

"Danielle! Danielle!"

"What? What's going on?"

"I heard kids out in the driveway. I went outside and I didn't recognize any of them. There were five. I saw our brother talking to an older woman at the bottom of the driveway, so I ran inside and asked Mom who was in the driveway. Then she said that was his *girlfriend*. It was our brother's new girlfriend and her kids."

"What? She has *five kids*?"

"Danielle, you aren't going to believe this. This lady ... she's like at least 45, older than Mom. She's fat and has a thick Hispanic accent that is hard to understand, and half of her kids are older than me!!!"

"His girlfriend is almost 30 years older than him *and* she has five kids? Are you SURE this is his girlfriend?"

"Um, yeah. And it gets even crazier. Mom is letting them live in the basement. All the kids are sleeping on cots. Then, I heard him talking to his friend ... about his girlfriend. He said having sex with her was like throwing a pencil down a hallway." *Holy hell, could this get any more disturbing???*

That my brother had mental issues had been obvious to me before, but now I was left wondering who was crazier — my brother or The Lady who gave birth to us? I was so glad to be gone. But so worried for my sister.

It was harder and harder to concentrate during my college classes or when I should be studying because I was so worried about my sister. Emotionally, I was still stuck in that house. I would have images of her being beaten to death. I would picture these five kids running around my yard, while my brother with serious "mommy issues" (having lost his father and seeing himself as the "man of the house") continued to mess up the way my sister thought about relationships. I wanted her out of there, but I also hated that my escape had done little to remove me completely from the toxic situation. It was like it would follow me anywhere.

 I hated that my escape had done little to remove
me completely from the toxic situation. It
was like it would follow me anywhere.

Living Like a Ghost

In 2006, Facebook was all the rage and while my roommates spent all day Sunday uploading their party pics from the night before, it seemed I was the only student at Endicott College (and possibly at any college in the United States!) without a Facebook page. I maintained my discipline about living like a girl in the witness-protection program. I didn't want my family to find me online or follow anything I was doing in my new life. I didn't want them to see me in my new *home*. I also didn't want to see what my friends were doing when they all got back together on holiday breaks and during the summer. It was all too emotional for me ... because I really missed them.

Endicott was my new home, but I would soon be homeless for the summer because they didn't allow freshmen to live on campus during the summer. The following years I would have the opportunity to pay to live on campus year-round, but this year I struggled coming up with a solution. I was about to get kicked out of my *new* home, but I couldn't (wouldn't!) go back to my *old* house.

I packed my car like everyone else and kept quiet about my summer plans. I tried to go unnoticed. I didn't have a plan at all but I had a 90-minute drive to figure something out. I assumed I should drive back to Leominster, because I didn't have another town to show up homeless to. I thought about everyone in my family. The Lady's side was out of the question and my Nana didn't have an extra bedroom. My dad's side was small, as we had lost two of my cousins to alcohol-related deaths before the age of 40. I showed up to my dad's sister's house. She was my aunt and godmother, and I was feeling lucky. She had an extra bedroom, and she knew I was just as clean as her. I figured if I offered to pay her rent and I was never home, it wouldn't be something she could refuse.

She was home. (Step 1 complete.) She was happy to see me. (A few extra points.) She was shocked that I stopped by for an unannounced visit. (Yeah, so was I. What the heck was I thinking?) Step 3: *ASK*.

I sat down at her kitchen table and awkwardly meandered the conversation to the fact that my car was packed, but I didn't have a place to live this summer. I was going back to my old jobs and I would never be home. "I will pay rent for your extra bedroom and I will be clean and quiet. You won't even know I am here."

"Oh, Danielle," she said. "My extra bedroom is filled with boxes from the kids. You know it's hard for me to get rid of their things. After your father's death, I lost both of my children, so I need to keep that extra room for storage."

"I don't even care about the boxes. I just need a bed and a shower. I won't even use your fridge because I can use the one at work."

"I can't have you here, Danielle. Why don't you go home to your house? I know your mom would love to have you back home. She just re-painted your room."

She delivered that news like it was joyful; I took it as an affront. "What? She repainted my room? Wow, she could hardly wait until I left, huh? What color did she paint it?"

"I believe she painted it a light pink."

"Oh WOWWWWW. My *least* favorite color. That sounds like something she would do. Don't you see what she does? I loved my yellow walls; she knew that. I picked the color out. She doesn't want me back and, trust me, that is the last place I would go back to. I am going to just live in my car. Thank you anyways. It was good to see you."

"Go home to your mother, Danielle."

"She isn't my mother. She abused us our whole lives and you want me to go back there? No fucking way. I am going to live in my car."

How is it that no one understood?

I didn't have anywhere to go or any place to park my car. Even though I loved my new home at college, I was already homeless again. In truth, I didn't mind living in my car, but I needed a shower. My thoughts were racing. *My own godmother won't even take me in. I lined up my jobs, so I have to be in Leominster, but I don't want to be back here. I have to be here one more summer, which wasn't part of my plan, and now I am living in my fucking car. AWESOME.*

Slumber Parties, Again

I called my friend Liesl, crying. Without hesitation, she offered for me to live with her this summer. When I reminded her that she didn't have an extra room in her house, she immediately answered, "No, it's fine. My bed is big enough and I don't mind sharing."

We spent the summer working our asses off, leaving work to run on the local running track late at night, and doing sit-ups on the carpet before we went to bed. We stayed up late together — something that we were both good at — but the mornings were rough, when she slept through her first five alarms and I was already cleaning the bathroom. We were in one bedroom upstairs, her older brother in another, and her youngest brother and his girlfriend in the last of the three bedrooms upstairs. Her dad stayed in the only bedroom downstairs, where he would generously take in as many of us orphans as he was asked to. If he knew someone who had a bad family life, he would take them in. He was among the first lenient and caring adults I ever knew.

Because I had mentally prepared myself to disappear and I was now back in Leominster unexpectedly, I didn't promote that I was back in town. I knew my friends were spending the summer reuniting, but I needed to distance myself. I would hide myself at work, feeling less lonely that I was with my best friend since 5th grade and seeing my boyfriend more now than when were at school. As much as I missed everyone, I was counting down until I could return home to Endicott, my new home for the next three years. I had never felt that kind of excitement before.

During that summer, as I did my best to be a ghost in my hometown, I would often get calls and text messages questioning if I was alive and where I had disappeared to. One childhood friend called and said a bunch of kids from my high school were together at a bonfire and my name was brought up. They hadn't seen me or heard about me since before we all left for college, so he called to see where "the girl who disappeared" had gone to. I played it off nonchalantly, because I couldn't exactly say that I was forcing myself to leave behind the friendships and parts of my life that I loved in order to survive.

In the fall, I returned to college, relieved that now I was "here to stay" for the next three years. While my course load increased, so did my anxiety about my sister. She now had her own cell phone, so she could text me and call me with more privacy, instead of only calling me from the house phone. I was in an elective class called World Disease, and I had just learned about toxic shock syndrome, which can be deadly if you leave a tampon in for too long. I became paranoid with this information when my sister stayed home from school with a high fever, a painful rash, and her period. The Lady refused to take her to the doctor, so I told her that if the symptoms continued for 24 hours, that I would drive back to Leominster and take her to the hospital.

I left Endicott on Saturday morning. I told my sister to ask The Lady for her health insurance card. That started a huge fight and when my sister revealed I was taking her to the hospital, The Lady refused to hand over the card. She said that I wasn't allowed near the house and I was not going to be picking her up. Well, I wouldn't be coming to the house either way. I told my sister I would call as I got closer and she needed to meet me at the end of the street for pick-up. But before I was able to make my call to tell her I was turning into the neighborhood, my phone rang.

I could hear screaming. I heard the sound of her feet hitting the pavement. I could hear heavy breathing.

"They are chasing me!! Hurry! Hurry!"

"Who is chasing you?"

"He is chasing me and Mom is in the car! Hurry, Danielle, hurry!"

I accelerated to 100 miles an hour down Union Street and made a wide, irresponsible right turn onto Birchcroft Road. I went even faster, looking for my sister so I could slam on my brakes and rescue her. As the road dipped before the bent corner that led to the house, I saw The Lady's car parked in the middle of the road. She was in the driver's seat and my brother was holding my sister, as she was screaming, crying and kicking, and he locked eyes with me, smiled, and threw her squirming body into the backseat, punching her back inside the car. I stared, forgetting that this wasn't a Bonnie and Clyde movie, as they both laughed, both driver and passenger ... as they drove down the street with my sister's face pressed against the glass, screaming my name.

I was unsure of where to go, but instead of following them, I decided to return to the scene where I assumed they would return. I went back to that house of horrors. I parked in front of the neighbor's house so that when they pulled around the corner, they wouldn't see my car. As soon as they pulled into the driveway, I was ready to face my two enemies — these two despicable humans who had just violently and corruptibly kidnapped my feverish, sick, terrified sister.

I waited, but the minutes felt like hours during which I received several call attempts from my sister. She would blurt out bits and pieces and then they would take her phone away. All I heard was, "they are taking me to Auntie Jeanne's." That was my cousin Kim's mom, but Kim was away at college. She lived a town over, and it was a half hour drive. I called my friend for advice and they helped me gain the courage to go to the police station.

The police knew my address by heart. Although we had often called them as kids looking for help, they were recently most familiar with my brother, who had racked up quite the record. I was instructed to wait outside the house and call them when the kidnappers returned. This was it. I would call, and both Bonnie and Clyde would be arrested for abuse.

Wow. It was FINALLY happening. I was relieved that the cycle was about to be broken, and that I was able to stop it. For my sister, and for myself.

I drove back to the house and waited. I couldn't stop crying. I was panicked — wondering what was happening to my sister, if she was hurt and if she was slowly dying from toxic shock syndrome. Then, another layer of panic. What would happen to my sister? I was living in a college dorm, not an apartment — I couldn't take her! WAIT. What if … FOSTER CARE.

The black SUV slithered into the driveway. I stayed in my car and waited for them to get inside. I kept calling my sister, but her phone was turned off and definitely stolen. I needed to get my sister out of that house before I called the police. A lot could happen in those 10 minutes.

I was more nervous to knock on my own front door than I was to show up at the police station. I had no idea what was going to happen, and I didn't have any back-up or pepper spray, just in case. I knocked on the door. There was complete silence. I waited. No answer. I knocked again, even louder. *Was my sister alive??* Then the door opened … it was The Lady.

She stood there behind the glass, her witch-like face with wrinkled skin, empty eyes, and frizzy hair. She stalled, in shock that it was me, back in the place I never wanted to return to. It had been three years since we'd seen each other. She opened the door a few inches and said nothing.

"Where is she," I stated firmly, without a question mark. I couldn't look at her. She was pure evil. I felt like my face would melt. I stared down at my feet, as I smelled the disgusting cigarette smoke escaping through the open door.

"She is upstairs."

"Let her out, NOW. The cops are on their way."

"The *cops*?"

"Yes. They are coming. You are going to get arrested. Now, let her out of this house right now before I come in there. You don't want to see me come in there."

She called her name. My sister came running down the stairs (13 hurried steps) and through the door and we ran — holding hands — onto the street and into my car. I was in control now. I hugged her and I pressed redial on my cell phone.

My sister looked like hell. Her face was red and puffy, and she had welts on her arms and legs. She told me that several family members were at Aunt Jeanne's. They took her phone away and told her she was never to talk to me or see me again. My older cousin tried to get her to pinky promise.

Three cops arrived. When they saw my sister, their faces sank. We talked outside by the mailbox before they went to the knock on the door. My sister and I waited and waited, but when they came back out, no one was in hand-cuffs. The police were alone.

"Hey! I thought they were getting arrested?"

"They both are denying any abuse."

"What do you mean they are denying abuse? Of *course* they are! That's what abusers do! I am telling you what I witnessed tonight, and what I have witnessed and experienced over the past 21 years! They NEED to be arrested. You told me ... you *lied* to me!"

"Ma'am, listen. We know your brother. We know this house. The problem is, we don't have a place for your sister to go. We just talked to your mother and your brother and things seem calm. They assured us they aren't going to abuse your sister tonight. We can work on something more permanent but, as for tonight, we don't have anywhere to put her."

"What about foster care? She is much safer in foster care!"

"The system is inundated, especially for teenagers. We just don't have a place to put her, so for now, she needs to stay here."

I couldn't breathe. I couldn't see. It felt like the salt from my tears had burned through my eyelids. Everything hurt.

"You aren't listening to me! She is NOT safe here! PLEASE. Do something!"

"We will work on a more permanent solution, but nothing is going to happen tonight."

I hated the cops. This was the first time I thought they would actually help me, and they failed me. They were weak, corrupt, and useless. I didn't like to beg, but I was willing to beg for this. I was at a loss.

Out of options, I took my sister back to my dorm room at Endicott College and monitored her rash and other symptoms through Sunday. Everything seemed to be clearing up and her fever was gone. If she didn't have school Monday, I would have kept her, but I didn't want her missing school. I took her to get a haircut and I bought her a winter jacket because she didn't have one that fit. On the drive back to Leominster, I made her promise me three things. I wanted her to work hard to get into foster care. If that meant have a friend hiding in her closet to witness or telling a teacher, I didn't care. *Make it happen, sister.* The second promise I made her agree to was getting straight A's. "If you get straight A's, I will take you shopping." I was not above bribery. The third promise was for her to call me every day. "I need you to check in with me every day. I don't care where you are or what you're doing. Keep to yourself, stay with friends as much as possible, and call me every single day."

She promised.

I dropped off my sister at the same dark door I couldn't imagine walking through again. Things stayed quiet for a little while. I was wrapping up my junior year of college with some peace and quiet, and then I received the phone call I had dreamt about my entire childhood: "I am in foster care."

Phases

Like phases of the moon,
there is a chase for fullness in my life,
only achieving it for a few moments
or just a few days among decades.
I am overcome by the need for a hundred years,
for more chances
to have a few more highs.
An addict of the full moon,
I find some days are dimmer,
others brighter,
as I pass quickly through the night sky.
While the full moon shines, there is a glow upon my face,
yet the hunger cravings persist during a waning crescent.
Happiness waxes and wanes
and I follow the light, giving chase to simple dreams.
Because I know my true self will shine
when I find my way to its core,
the center of all. The light within me.

Hunger

I couldn't help but feel a deep sense of retroactive envy and then the truest form of explosive joy. My sister had achieved my dream. She made it to safety. It was all I ever wanted but instead, the cops never listened, and I was there for 18 long, miserable years — crying myself to sleep, hiding, running, yelling, fighting, not breathing. Now, she got what I fought for. These were my immediate and honest thoughts. After I talked myself off the roller coaster of envy and self-pity, I could happily accept that the seeds I planted more than a decade ago were now like Jack's fabled bean stalk, growing just in time to reach, grab, and rescue my sister.

> I couldn't help but feel a deep sense of retroactive envy and then the truest form of explosive joy. My sister had achieved my dream. She made it to safety.

"You're safe now," I told her with glee. "You are going to have great parents and you will have family dinners and maybe even vacations! Wow, I am so happy for you! You did it. You made it!"

"Well, I am in a temporary home. They are nice, but they are very strict. I can't use the phone every day and I only have five minutes on this call, but I wanted to call you and tell you that I'm in foster care and I am OK. I will call you as soon as I can."

"What? Wait. Can I talk to them and see if we can at least talk longer? I still need to know what happened! How you got there."

"I can't; I will get in trouble. I'm not supposed to talk to any family members, but I lied and told them I was calling a friend. I will call you as soon as I can. I love you."

"Call me as soon as you can. I am very worried now and I need to know where you are going! I love you too. I am very proud of you. You did it."

New Routines, New Connections, New Challenges

Living at Endicott was like living at an all-inclusive resort. I had an ocean view every day, whether it was from my dorm window or my classroom window. We only got a few actual beach days during the Massachusetts school year, but my summer days were as if I had my very own private beaches, all at my fingertips and a simple walk across the street. There was silence here, the most sought-after blessing of my life. I could feel my old wounds healing, with my body on the sand, absorbing the warmth and love from the sun.

 There was silence here, the most sought-after blessing of my life. I could feel my old wounds healing.

I nannied during my college summers and after school during the school year. I met two wonderful families on Craigslist and I took my responsibilities seriously: keeping education, fun activities, and well-balanced meals as a priority for the children. During the summers, I was with Courtney and Colby 50 hours a week. We would walk to the library, go to their aunt's pool, make sandcastles on the beach, ride bikes, see movies, and organize day trips. I would plan the whole week out in terms of meals and weather — with arts-and-crafts on rainy days and making sure the kids' plates always had a fruit and a vegetable. I loved every second of it. Against all odds, I had a maternal instinct. I would often think of The Lady's failures as a mother and how I would be the complete opposite. I was going to be the best mom; that was one thing in my future I was sure about.

Every Friday, I would deposit my cash in the bank, stockpiling my summer money to get me through the rest of the school year (when I would not be able to work as much). Between my senior internship at an interior design firm in the south end of Boston, schoolwork, and work, I couldn't be on the college dance team for my final year. I also had my senior thesis project to focus on and I wanted it to be the best project I ever completed, because this was it. I could not leave Endicott without knowing that I gave my absolute best to everything I did. I knew I would live with regret with anything less, and this education was too expensive to not give it 100%.

The biggest decision of my life was waiting for me. It was time to decide where I would move after graduation. Now, I was in control, and I could live wherever I wanted. I had barely been across the Massachusetts state border. When it came to the United States and the broader world, I *knew* nothing and I had *seen* nothing. Yet. It was time for a change of scenery. I never did fit into the grumpy Massachusetts crowd. I was eager to plan my next disappearance.

 When it came to the United States and the broader world, I knew nothing and I had seen nothing. Yet. It was time for a change of scenery.

In high school, I would always bring maps to school. I remember sitting in Latin class one day, circling the southern town names that sounded cool, as I dreamt of my Birchcroft Road escape. I was always interested in California, Georgia, North Carolina, and Florida. I knew nothing about these states but listened to my intuition; I experienced warm and fuzzy feelings when I stared at my map. When I first revisited looking at all the states, as my college adventure was coming to an end, I wanted to choose the furthest place possible, so I convinced my friend Liesl to visit San Diego with me. She was interested in applying for graduate schools and I was interested in moving far away to a place with beaches. Her mom paid for our hotel accommodations and we spent four days scouting the area, riding the metro and touring apartments. The rent in San Diego was certainly intimidating for two college students. Everything seemed more expensive in southern California. The only areas that we felt we could possibly afford didn't appear safe. The beaches were behind huge parking lots and filled with overwhelming crowds. As much as we tried to convince ourselves that this was an exciting escape plan, the city was too big, too expensive, and less quaint than I wanted. Time to go back to the map.

I looked at geography, latitude, and longitude. I dragged my finger horizontally across the map, starting at the San Diego coastline, moving east, and ending at Wilmington, North Carolina. I didn't know anything about Wilmington, but I saw it had several beaches. It was in one of the states that had always intrigued me. It was still on the east coast, which seemed to be where my heart was, but it was far enough away from Leominster, Massachusetts — 800 miles, to be exact. I looked up Wilmington on Wikipedia, the world's most reliable source, and discovered that the town had history, charm, and those live oaks that overhang the streets with Spanish moss cascading down. It was a town with people who loved to be outdoors. There were horse-drawn carriage tours through the historic district downtown and it was filmed as the beautiful backdrop of two of my favorite shows: *Dawson's Creek* and *One Tree Hill*. I was sold. I nodded and said to myself, *"LET'S DO IT!!!"*

It really was that easy. I didn't have any money left for scouting, so I decided to take the plunge and go for the move. If it didn't work out, I could always move again. My nerves hid in the shadows of my excitement for my secret move to North Carolina. I had to start researching apartments and jobs. I was going from being a "New England Masshole" to a southern belle (minus the belle). Exploring a new place was like locking the door to my childhood and throwing away the key. I could move to a new place and no one would know anything about me or my family. It was a fresh start at life, where I was in control of creating my destiny — free from where I had come from.

I would miss our New England trees, which showed like an autumn rainbow against the blue sky when they appeared, because the cold gray skies were wicked — I mean wicked bad. Although my student loan debt was racking up, my food at the time seemed free, which made it taste even better. The cafeteria salad bar made life too easy, but I was hooked on vegetables, which seemed like a miracle since I can't remember eating one as a child (except for iceberg lettuce). I would use my student food plan's "flex dollars" on large pizzas from our downtown favorite, Little Italy, which had a sweet, secret sauce recipe. I knew that once I started paying for my food (without the assistance of federal student loans), I wouldn't be able to support these frequent large pizza orders. Times, they were a-changin'.

 Exploring a new place was like locking the door to my childhood and throwing away the key. I could move to a new place and no one would know anything about me or my family. It was a fresh start at life, where I was in control of creating my destiny — free from where I had come from.

This would be the last sneaky winter, where our ponds would freeze over just in time for ice skating and hot chocolate. Our eyelashes would freeze walking to class and the snow slush would wet our shoes and the bottom of our pants, so we would sit through our 3-hour studio classes with that Massachusetts attitude, pretending we didn't want to be there but secretly knowing that next year, we would probably miss this.

I continued to sleep less while keeping up my grades to my standards and keeping my friendships strong. This would be my final three seasons here and part of me wanted life to slow down. The pressure I put on myself was always immense but I knew that finding a job, renting an apartment, and paying back my student loan debt would make college pressure seem like a piece of cake. With this in mind, I stared as the leaves changed and as the snow fell. I went apple picking for my last time in New England. I was able to appreciate the winter's bitter, icy air for the first time, as my last time.

A Beginning and an End — Farewell to Massachusetts

The seasons swept me away, through four years at Endicott College, until I blinked and realized that it was now time to really disappear — to a different state, in a secret town, far away, where not one family member could find me, as long as my sister kept my secret. As it turned out, my sister's foster care experience wasn't what we had envisioned. She bounced through several temporary homes and ended up in a group home as her final destination. From what I remember, there were six or eight teenage girls in one room, all sleeping on bunk beds, while the foster mom kept all of her other bedrooms open, in a large home. My sister had more phone access now, so I could talk her through transitioning to a new school in a new town and talk her off the ledge when the other girls would steal her clothes.

The Massachusetts Department of Social Services (DSS), now known as the Department of Children and Families, was doing regular check-ins and everything seemed to be acceptable until my sister got pneumonia. The cold nights with little heat didn't help and there was no one rushing her to the doctor. When DSS picked my sister up, she was 90 pounds, frail, hungry, and extremely sick. They removed her from the foster home and there were no available spots for a teenage female foster kid. DSS ended up returning my sister back home, but removed legal custody from The Lady, so my sister became a free agent (i.e., an emancipated minor), with more leverage than ever before.

I was devastated by the prospect of my sister going back to our mother and brother, and I fought for her to stay in the group home. I told her I would talk to the foster mom and all the girls and make sure she was fed and treated better. I was stubborn and even though she would be 18 in a few years, I didn't want The Lady to get her back, because she didn't deserve her. My sister was worn down and desperate. She wanted her bed, her school, and her friends back. I wanted her to live my dream for me and that dream didn't have this ending.

 My sister was worn down and desperate. She wanted her bed, her school, and her friends back. I wanted her to live my dream for me and that dream didn't have this ending.

The ending I pictured was a "happily ever after." I envisioned a warm, loving home with two working parents, a dog, a cat, and a few siblings. This fictional family I imagined for her wouldn't let her walk a mile to the bus stop in the rain, sleet or snow — they would drive her. They would give her birthday parties and have family game nights. They would do weekend trips and host big Thanksgivings with a variety of handmade pies. They would attend parent-teacher conferences, check her report cards, and even sched-ule college tours. She would have scheduled haircuts, dentist appointments, and therapy sessions. Christmases would be filled with sweet traditions and the smells of a fresh-cut tree, sugar cookies, and cinnamon pine cones. I thought that if she got out of the house on Birchcroft Road, her life on the other side would be normal and safe. I thought it would have love and hugs. I thought they would keep her out of trouble.

My fantasy evolved into heartbreak and I mourned the loss of the opportunity I always imagined as "the opportunity of a lifetime," for the both of us. I wasn't equipped for this. I was too invested and the more invested I was, the more toxicity traveled into my dorm room and robbed me of being freed, in this beautiful place that I loved so much. It was time to distance myself from my toxic former "home life" — even if that meant distancing myself from my sister.

I tried to focus my stress only on school. When my sister would call with bad family news, I would politely ask her to not share these things with me any longer. Sometimes she would blurt things out and I would mentally drug myself with amnesia. I didn't want to hear about The Lady's screaming fights, our brother's crack spoons in the trash, or his newest arrest for abusing his girlfriend. I didn't want to hear about how she got nothing for Christmas or how the family dog was having uncontrollable bowel movements in my old bedroom and no one was cleaning it up. I didn't want to listen to the constant complaints about a lack of groceries in the house or how The Lady was still sleeping on the brown sofa, where she spent her days and nights. I would suffocate in the thoughts of a smoke-filled house with piles of dog feces on the carpet next to hoarding piles of mail and garbage and clothes and god-knows-what. I couldn't think about a drug-addicted, sociopathic criminal living in the basement with prostitutes. This was what it had come to and I didn't want to know about it anymore. I needed to move on. And I needed to *move*.

Disappearance Day, Take 2

I was so nervous that I was feeling nauseated, shaking in silence underneath my graduation gown. A professor walked over to our alphabetical line of classmates in the Endicott gymnasium.

He asked, full of pride and support for us all, "What are you doing after graduation?"

Graduates were mumbling about all variations of moving back home — back home for the summer and focusing on job searches, back home until the economy gets better, back home to work one last summer as a camp counselor.

He turned to me, was it obvious that I was avoiding the question and turning the other way, as if I didn't hear the question. Perhaps he thought I was shy or deferential, and wanted to ensure to include me in the celebratory, forward-looking conversation.

"What about you? What are your plans post-graduation?"

"I am moving to North Carolina."

"Oh wow, what's in North Carolina?"

"The beach. I am moving to a beach town called Wilmington."

"Do you have family there?"

"No." (*Hell no.*)

"Do you have a job?"

"Not yet. I tried, but no one answered my messages or emails."

"Well, it sounds like an adventure. When are you leaving?"

"Today."

I gave all eight of my graduation tickets to my friend Caitlin, who had a big family. I didn't have anyone to give my tickets to. I didn't need anyone to be proud of me, but I was proud of myself for what I had accomplished.

 I gave all eight of my graduation tickets to my friend Caitlin, who had a big family. I didn't have anyone to give my tickets to. I didn't need anyone to be proud of me, but I was proud of myself for what I had accomplished.

That was a hard feeling for me, but I felt like I had grown and given so much in my college years. I had worked harder than ever before — harder than I probably should have. (Because, for me, college was for skipping showers, meals, and sleep so I could do my best at everything and everyone I had committed to.) My classmates once found me sleeping on a sofa in the library on their way to class. Since I had calculated that each class cost several hundred dollars and I was so determined to make something of myself, I was proud of the work I had done the past four years. I was exhausted, but proud.

On May 15, 2010, I graduated from Endicott College as the first college graduate in my family. I was surprised that "cum laude" (with honors!) was read after my name. I had taken Latin in high school, but never learned what these fancy words meant when attached to a diploma, so I asked the person next to me. It means you had a grade point average between 3.5 and 3.7. I graduated with a 3.6.

After graduation, families filled the streets, taking pictures, handing out flowers, and giving goodbye hugs. I watched through my rearview mirror, as I pulled out of my townhouse (what we called the upscale dorms on campus) and drove down the hill, then past the football field, the cafeteria, and the pond in my Plymouth Neon, packed to the roof with everything I owned (minus winter clothes and boots), to a historic coastal town in North Carolina … called Wilmington.

This was my last day being trapped in Massachusetts, and I was finally being set free. I had $900 in my bank account when I embarked on that 16-hour drive. I arrived at my new home — an apartment complex called the Colonial Grand — and pulled into a parking spot. That car never started back up again. I guess this was where I was meant to land.

On My Own

My apartment didn't have cockroaches, which was my biggest fear, and it actually looked exactly like it did in the photos on the internet. Thank goodness! I had my very own one-bedroom apartment with a balcony and a fireplace, and access to a community pool and a laundry facility. It had a sliding door and a bedroom window, allowing the daylight to pour through. The walls were white and the carpet was clean. The doorway didn't feel dark or heavy, and the air smelled like fresh paint. It was perfect.

Everything looked different in Wilmington. The grocery stores were Food Lion and Harris Teeter instead of Market Basket and Shaws. I felt like I was in a different country — the roads were double-laned, the people spoke with southern drawls, and restaurants offered sweet tea instead of water. It was a different culture, which made me feel uneasy, yet equally excited. I was far away from the toxic family I left behind, and I felt further, safer, and freer than ever before. I was comforted by the presence of a Walmart and a Dollar Tree. The biggest change was in my chest. I could breathe again. My chest wasn't tight and my nightmares subsided. I felt like all the negative energy that had attached to me in Massachusetts wasn't here in North Carolina. I was really alone now and instead of this sudden reality bringing loneliness, it brought a lightness I had never felt before.

> I felt like I was in a different country — the roads were double-laned, the people spoke with southern drawls, and restaurants offered sweet tea instead of water. It was a different culture, which made me feel uneasy, yet equally excited. I was far away from the toxic family I left behind, and I felt further, safer, and freer than ever before.

It was time to become an independent adult, without roommates or a dictated schedule. But first there were two things I needed: a car and a job. I couldn't get a job without the car, but I couldn't get a car without the job, so I called the Honda dealership and a man named Greg answered the phone. I told Greg my predicament and, as a father of four, he offered to pick me up from my apartment and take me to the dealership to find a new vehicle. Why the hell was I going with a car salesman, who I didn't know, alone? Well, I was desperate. I had bills to pay. The day I left Endicott, the accrued interest on my unsubsidized student loans added $20,000 to my debt. I had $100,000 over my head and, with the way interest multiplies, this was just a starting point.

Greg — my new car salesman hero — pulled some strings and got me in a slightly used 2010 Honda Civic with 16,000 miles on it. It was $14,000 and

I was approved for the loan (miracle of miracles!) because I had earned some credit from paying my cell phone bills on time and because I had a $1,000-limit Bank of America credit card. I'll never forget having applied for that credit card when I was heading to college because a kind and clairvoyant bank teller said it would help build me credit. To this day, I am grateful for that banker. The only thing I knew about credit growing up was that we didn't have it, and that it took seven years to get it back after my parents went bankrupt.

Holy shit! I was driving a new car. It was a nice car. It was an expensive car. It was shiny, with four doors and power windows. The dash glowed in LED blue at night. The odometer and speedometer were digital. It was a weird, Carolina blue, but I didn't care because I couldn't believe that this was MY car.

I sold my Neon for $200 on Craigslist and I felt like a millionaire, but without evidence to back it up. I had a Walmart futon in my living room with a $35 coffee table, a zebra-print rug, mismatched pillows, a $10 yard-sale desk (covered in red, papier-mâché), an IKEA dresser, and a wooden platform with an 8-inch foam mattress. I thought I was living like a queen.

I found a job at Ashley Furniture, which was exactly a mile from my apartment, and I figured furniture was a close start to working in design. I worked there for two months before my dream job popped up in my email. I became a designer for a custom decorating company. My clients were mostly retirees living in beautiful, gated communities. At first, I worked in the Wilmington market and then I took over the Myrtle Beach market,

First apartment in Wilmington, NC, living like a queen

where I would drive anywhere from 4-6 hours a day, designing high-end soft goods, where the trunk of my Honda Civic became my fabric library and I became a professional designer with an office, a secretary, and an installer. In addition to learning different design styles and all about fabric, I learned how to generate leads, gain referrals, pre-qualify clients, manage my time, delegate work to a secretary, receive warehouse inventory, track orders, install jobs, and, most importantly, how to connect with my clients and create something special for them. I had a profession and I was in heaven.

I still felt the lingering exhaustion from those college all-nighters. I was so burnt out from those four years of college and from the 18 years in that house. It was like I was still recuperating.

I worked a typical 40-hour work week, but I spent about 20 hours a week at the pool or the beach, lying in the sun, mostly alone, doing absolutely nothing other than letting the silence, sand, water, and sun heal me. At night, I would read or watch reality TV, everything from *The Voice* to *Keeping Up with the Kardashians* to *Real Housewives* marathons. There was no better cure for making me feel better about myself. Watching these empty lives filled with drama boosted my self-esteem and made me hate plastic surgery. The theme I found in watching these shows was that no woman seemed to love herself. Or maybe that was just what I noticed because that was what I felt.

Perhaps the first step in learning to love myself was in allowing myself to be loved by a pet. So in my first year on my own, I rescued a puppy. Honestly, I still can't believe how my heart gave into this, but I suddenly had all this spare time and room in my heart to try out the practice of love and nurturing — something I had never really learned. While helping my friend Jess search for a dog for herself on Petfinder, I saw this little face, teddy-bear colored, attached to a little three-pound body that fit in the palm of a hand. I looked at the three photos of him, and my OCD be damned, I needed him. There was a litter of four puppies, rescued from the scene of a car accident where the mama dog was hit by a car. The face I fell in love with belonged to the runt of the litter.

I was about to become a dog lover — someone with a new relationship with animals that eclipsed my experience of "dog ownership" to that point. I grew up with a dog who was a German Shepherd/Rottweiler mix and there was hardly any attachment there. Looking back now, I understand (and mourn for the fact) that we were taught to keep ourselves disconnected from the dog, as he stayed outside on his chain between two trees, was too forceful to walk, and did not cuddle — not because he wasn't a good dog, but because no one had ever invited him to be adored and cared for as he deserved. (I could relate.) Up until my mid-20s, I always considered it "weak" when people cried about their pets passing away — because, in my house, our pets were just accessories to make us seem more normal to anyone taking a close look. We were a family of five with a colonial-style house, a dog, a cat, and a backyard pool. It sounded good on paper, but it was like we were playing a bad game of poker, bluffing our way through every step, presenting a fake perfect world to everyone else, but really it was a chaotic, dark, dirty house without love.

But now, after I had been away from my family for a few years and was opening my heart and mind to a more functional life, I was able to find myself smitten. This little puppy face — wow. It kept staring at me. I thought about this picture for days, and I kept coming back to the computer to pull up the photos on Petfinder. And then I made the phone call. For some reason, something was telling me that I was meant to be his mom and he was meant to be my baby dog, whether it made sense or not. I named him Cooper and he quickly became the best part of my life. This was

The day I adopted Cooper

the first time I had ever felt something like this, and it was the best feeling I had ever had. I had unconditional love for someone, and it was reciprocated right back.

Making Friends and Making My Way

Eventually, I made some friends in Wilmington and I traded in my extended alone time for more social time. I was going to play team trivia every

Thursday at a local hangout and I made friends at the apartment complex swimming pool. My friends and I would go out every Saturday — sometimes dancing, but most times to a "dueling pianos" bar, followed by shooting pool at the oldest pool hall in the United States. And then there was my personal favorite pastime: post office pizza. Post office pizza is just how it sounds. We would get pizza and eat it on the stone stairs of the post office. There was some amount of rebellion or taboo to this, eating at a government building at night, watching all the drunk people meander by, while the homeless men lingered closely, lured by the smell of the pizza. It was a simple weekly joy. Plus, the pizza was the highlight of my night, seeing as I wasn't drinking alcohol and food, instead, became my weekend reward.

For the first three years in Wilmington, I worked my way up at work until I reached a point where I had maxed out at my potential with the company and I didn't want to travel anymore (I hated leaving Cooper). Sometimes I would take my fur-baby on the road with me or hide him under my desk in Myrtle Beach, but I didn't feel right about leaving him home alone all day, especially if I wanted to go out on Thursday for trivia. It was time for me to look locally for a new job. But this wasn't Boston and there weren't any large interior design firms in the area. Actually, there weren't many firms at all. After becoming desperate and applying for any job in just about any field, I had followed the path of yet another Craigslist ad.

There was a newer business that had opened downtown in an old bank building on a cobblestone street, and it was just across the way from my favorite spot: the post office. The owners had opened a design store as their retirement business, and they were looking for an interior designer to work with clients outside of the store and help build their brand and business within the community. I had the confidence that I could succeed with this opportunity and I felt ready. I had rested for over three years and I was ready to be a successful over-achiever who would "become someone" — someone whose name was known by others (and for reasons other than that she lived at the house where the police were always showing up). I wanted to do big things. I had always felt that I was made for big things. Sometimes I would convince myself that I was going to change the world, but I didn't know how. I just knew I had it in me, which after all I had been through, was a kind of confidence that was nothing short of a miracle.

I had always felt that I was made for big things.

The business owners must have believed I had potential too, because I got the job. Here I was — 24 years old, parking my Honda Civic in a downtown garage, walking on main streets in the heart of Wilmington, with my $25 purse, Payless shoes, and my clearance rack JCPenney work pants (which had dragged heels because I was too short and too poor to get them hemmed). The couple I worked for seemed to favor me over the other designer they hired, and this created a one-sided animosity war that left me with enough hints for me to not want to be around the office, so I started finding ways to get me out of the office. I think I was conditioned to find escapes. I could easily disappear without realizing that this was a learned behavior from my past.

I started calling every rep for every designer product I could find. My first appointment was with a Benjamin Moore paint rep. His name was Adam and I asked Adam who the best builders were, who my competition was and, naturally, who the best painter was. Adam told me to call a woman named Lucinda. He repeated, *"You have to meet Lucinda."*

I couldn't picture what Lucinda would look like. I had never met a Lucinda before. I left her an awkward voicemail and figured she would never call me back. The next day, I called again and left another voicemail. Then, Lucinda called me back. We arranged a meeting in the McDonald's parking lot, in the town of Southport, outside a gated retirement community named St. James — where I had previously worked with clients. She sounded friendly and enthusiastic, so when she told me I should look for her minivan and she would take me to some of her jobs, I didn't think twice. I was excited to meet a Lucinda.

On the day I met Lucinda in her minivan, I discovered that she and I were kindred spirits. She was 20 years older than me, but we shared similar physical and professional attributes. We even wore the same eyeliner. We rode to several homes where her crews were working and it was obvious that her business — Coastal Painting — was a successful company. There were handfuls of crews working across several projects, both in new construction and remodels. I was impressed.

Lucinda shared her story with me that day. She and her husband, Eugene, had owned a very successful scrap metal business in upstate New York. They could have retired when they moved down here to the Wilmington area, but they were too young and would have been bored, so they started investing money in the strong real estate market by building a painting company and flipping houses. They were turning houses into homes, and it was akin to what I'd always dreamed of doing since discovering interior design while watching *Trading Spaces* with my cousin. Lucinda and Eugene owned several houses when the economy crashed in 2007-2008. They had many open mortgages and when the property values started dropping to the point that mortgage notes were upside down, Lucinda and Eugene lost almost everything.

It was 2013 when I met Lucinda, so it had only been a few years since she was in a grocery store with her children and she didn't have enough money to pay for milk and toilet paper. The man behind her helped pay the balance she owed. She was personally painting homes, she was cleaning houses, and even mowing lawns. She was doing whatever it took, but one of their builders declared bankruptcy, while still owing them $40,000. That was the straw that broke the camel's back.

Lucinda and Eugene went from having it all to losing it all, then to regaining what they had and working toward having it all again. *Wow, this could happen to me. I could have it all.* I was willing to work harder than ever before, and I was inspired by someone who told me that this area of North Carolina had immense potential with the way construction was before the crash and the way it was building up to that point again. Lucinda told me I needed to start networking to do anything that could help me build connections and get my name out there. She told me to join one of her networking groups — called K&M Speed Networking — so that is exactly what I did.

Networking

I went home after that first day with Lucinda, and I remember feeling like my fire was back. I was making a base salary with a tiered commission structure, and I wanted to "become someone" with something, which included a better place to live. I felt like a con artist in many ways — through my employer, I was charging $90 an hour to wealthy and successful clients in high-end homes in gated communities and here I was living in an apartment, sleeping on an 8-inch piece of foam. What if they asked about my house that I didn't have? I couldn't lie to them, but I was embarrassed for them to ever know or ask about the truth. I needed to get out of here. I wanted to keep climbing.

I remember coming home and sitting on the edge of my sofa with my laptop on my lap, making the phone call to join K&M. I was going to be a professional "networker," whatever that meant. I put the meeting schedule in my paper calendar, and I checked my bank account to see if I could manage to buy a few new outfits. I had to look the part and I was going to follow the words of the wise: "You just need to fake it until you make it."

I also started to research local magazines. I loved to write, and I wanted to start writing about design. I found a local magazine, *Wrightsville Beach Magazine,* which ran a monthly publication based around a center spread called the Home of Distinction. I looked for a contact and emailed the editorial manager, Marimar. She asked if I had any writing samples. I explained to her that I didn't have any editorial writing experience, but I had the design education and background. I offered to create my own writing sample, using photographs of my recently completed projects. I studied previous Home of Distinction articles and I even mocked the graphic design for my sampling because I needed to prove that I wanted this opportunity more than anyone else. It wasn't about the $140 a month I would get paid (though that was nice); it was about fulfilling my love for writing, embarking on personal growth, and learning who was in the design game. I wanted to be the behind-the-scenes secret agent who was meeting all the builders, architects, and designers. I wanted to see who I wanted to work with and who I didn't want to work with. I wanted to see who my competition was and how I could stand out against them.

I wanted to be the behind-the-scenes secret agent who was meeting all the builders, architects, and designers. I wanted to see who I wanted to work with and who I didn't want to work with. I wanted to see who my competition was and how I could stand out against them.

Marimar hired me as the design writer for *Wrightsville Beach Magazine*. She gave me a chance. She sat me down with my first article and made red pen marks across my printed-out pages. I listened to everything she said and I promised that I would work hard to never disappoint. In fact, I was going to impress her each and every month. Through this journalism opportunity, I saw incredible homes — on the ocean, on islands, and along the intra-coastal waterways. I met self-made, successful homeowners and I loved hearing their stories. I met the builders, architects, and designers, humbly introducing myself as "the writer" for the magazine's feature, keeping the secret that I was also an interior designer. To them, I was just the writer, and I preferred to keep it that way.

I began networking — a term I had to learn and a business strategy I wanted to master because I saw the personal and professional value in it. Because I was able to connect with new people, make friends, and build profes-sional relationships, I felt that networking gave me that sense of connec-tion that I was longing for after being in a new city and state for over three years, where I had made just a small group of friends. I was a nobody. I was average now, but I was never average before North Carolina. I always had a huge friend group and I thrived off being overcommitted and being pulled in multiple directions. During my chaotic childhood, I was a social butterfly despite the odds. Now that I was free and safe, I was living a quieter, more anonymous life. The freedom and safety were incredible, but I was ready to be known, be seen, and be social again.

As I was finding my way as a young adult, it was fascinating to look back on the positive (outside-of-the-house) parts of my childhood, where I was engaged, joyful, and always on some sort of stage. In middle school, I was singing with my trio The Kandi Kiss Kids and performing throughout the year. Still in those middle grades, I started my student-government career as secretary. I was involved in the gifted-and-talented program and Future Problem Solvers club; danced in ballet, tap, jazz and pointe classes; worked my paper route on the weekday afternoons and the weekend mornings, babysat on weekend nights and used every extra hour for homework and being a social butterfly. I would schedule time with each friend group, making sure I would rotate my time evenly so I could maintain all of my friendships. I took this seriously because I felt alive when I was connecting with people.

I felt alive when I was connecting with people.

In high school, I was once again the secretary of student government, and I planned every fundraiser, class trip, and two proms. I danced three nights a week. I played tennis (which was almost every day after school) and I worked the nights I wasn't at dance and had fun working weekend doubles to get my 40 hours a week. In college, I was managing 40 hours of class time each week, practicing and performing with the dance team, working, and of course keeping my time with friends as a priority. I was always using every hour of my time to make myself feel connected, productive, and have a sense of achievement so that I didn't have a spare second to get distracted with where I came from, who I came from, or who I really was. I must be a bad person, I thought. I did and said horrible things in that house. I needed to stay busy, so I didn't have to remember those things.

 I was always using every hour of my time to make myself feel connected, productive, and have a sense of achievement so that I didn't have a spare second to get distracted with where I came from, who I came from, or who I really was.

My first few years in Wilmington were important for me to refill my emotional tank and my energy stores. I was burnt out from 22 years of healthy and unhealthy stress, both of which I had become accustomed to, where I was now conditioned to function at a certain pace with a full plate of distractions. I didn't exercise, I watched way too much television, and I was hanging out with people who drank more than even the partiers I knew in college. I guess being burnt out meant I lowered my standards for myself. When my plate was not full, I was lazy and not contributing to the world like I wanted to, or like I knew I was meant to do. I started filling my plate again, but it didn't matter how many people, events, or accomplishments I added — I still wasn't full. I had never felt emptier. It was the same spiritual hunger I always had, which I could never seem to feed.

By this point in my life, my relationship with my sister had taken a turn. She stopped listening to me and instead of telling me the truth, she would rather ignore my calls and let our relationship crumble. She was going through a phase of self-destruction, and I didn't know how to help her. She was dying her hair a different color every week. She was partying hard, with the wrong crowd, and had started dating a heroin addict. I realized that her heart was in the right place, but she was too young and naïve to realize that she couldn't cure her past by saving an addict in her present. She was creating my worst nightmare by eroding my ability to salvage one family relationship. I could not lose her too.

 My sister was partying hard, with the wrong crowd, and had started dating a heroin addict. I realized that her heart was in the right place, but she was too young and naïve to realize that she couldn't cure her past by saving an addict in her present.

When her relationship with her boyfriend ended, my sister began to unravel and to lash out at me. Our relationship was struggling hard; she had joined the family by calling me a bitch. At some point, it was easier for me to not speak to her at all. Then one day, after several months of not speaking, my phone rang several times. I was visiting Liesl in Washington, DC, and I didn't see the missed calls until we left a museum. I texted my sister to make sure the calls were meant for me. She followed up with a series of text messages, saying that she had been raped, that she was pregnant, and that she needed help. The problem was, my sister rarely told the truth, especially during this time in her life, so I couldn't believe a word that she said. The drama (and the trauma) was incessant.

Becoming Myself Again

I had built a small, but strong clientele base through the design shop where I worked. I was working seven days a week and pulling all-nighters because I was desperate to impress clients with the amount of work product I could turn around in a small timeframe. Between working, networking, exercising, and expanding my friend group, I was becoming myself again.

Now, I was networking in the morning, at lunch, and at night. I was meeting people of all ages, backgrounds, and professions. I had met a man named Bruce who really got me thinking. He and his wife, Marge, were the idealistic "happy couple" who had been married more than 40 years and were just smitten with one another. They were a good deal older than me but I connected with them on so many levels, finding them to be so young in spirit. Bruce was a mentor in K&M — my local networking group — and he had written a book on networking. He seemed to have a great deal of knowledge about the intersection of passion and people. We had these two things in common, so I wanted to learn from his wisdom.

Bruce was an instant mentor to me and he had quickly given me two pushes: one push was toward getting a Facebook page (just a personal profile) and the other push was to read a book called *The Passion Test* by Janet Bray Attwood and Chris Attwood. I did not want my family to find me, so I had never set up a Facebook profile, even when everyone else had … and when it was fast becoming the standard way of keeping in touch with friends. I had made it through college without Facebook and because I'd never been sucked into the habit, I found the very concept of a Facebook presence as a time-wasting distraction and an opportunity for people to portray fake happiness to all their fake friends. Then Bruce reiterated to me how important a social media presence was when it came to networking a business. After many back-and-forth conversations, I finally gave in and established a Facebook profile under the code name "PCDG Danielle."

Then I started skimming the pages of *The Passion Test*. Though I had already identified my passion, that didn't mean my life was on track to fulfill my passions to their fullest extent … and it didn't mean I had yet discovered my life's *purpose*. The book gave me assignments. I did everything from creating vision boards to writing passion cards and putting them in my wallet and on my fridge. I learned about the law of attraction. For months, I read these positive, inspiring statements every day off my fridge door, one of which included one note card that said, "I want to change the lives of others through design while owning my own interior design firm." The point of this "passion card" exercise was that the more I focused on my passions, the more ingrained they became in my mind. As a result, when I was faced with a decision, I would be more likely to stay aligned with my passions.

When you are clear, what you want will show up in your life (but only to the extent you are clear). I was ready to get crystal clear.

What Had I Done?

I had reached my first six months at work and, coincidentally, it was the first time I had earned a commission bonus. It was perfect timing because I needed a new laptop. I was doing all my design projects on my college laptop and it was about to explode. Between some design deadline and a designer charity event for Habitat for Humanity, I had not slept in two days. It was the first of the month, when I was supposed to get paid. I was feeling eager and anxious. I was only paid once a month, which made budgeting more difficult, but I was also a 1099 independent contractor, which also meant I had to pay my own taxes and didn't have the various protections of employees. I never understood why I had to ask to be paid each month (I guess they thought it was my job as a contractor to "invoice" them, which I now realize it probably was) but I absolutely hated asking. They knew how much they agreed to pay me and how much work I had done each month, so cutting my check should have been a matter of routine. It was uncomfortable to have to nudge them for my money and always felt a little sketchy to me. Being young and wanting to avoid conflict, I would always let the discomfort and worry sit for a few days before I brought it up to the business owner, and I would be paid late once again. But this time, my IT guy (a technologist I met at my networking group) said if I waited to get my files transferred to a new computer much longer, I would lose everything on my laptop.

It was May 1, 2014. I was 25 years old when I asked Lonnie about receiving my monthly check with my first bonus commission and she replied with an upbeat comment about wanting to go out to dinner to celebrate my first bonus. I replied with gratefulness, telling her that I appreciated the offer but, if possible, I wanted to celebrate later so that I could go to sleep after work. I was running on fumes. She refuted, explaining that to receive my paycheck, I needed to meet her and her husband, Will, for dinner.

I cannot explain how tired I was. The adrenaline had died off and, as much as I needed the meal, I would have gone to bed hungry. This, incidentally, is a tradeoff I would rarely make — I was always the hungriest person I knew! But I was going to have to push through the crushing fatigue because my employers said they wanted me to meet at the country club where they held a social membership. This is where they met with me upon my official hire. I felt out of place and uncomfortable, but I couldn't figure out why.

I arrived to find a stack of papers on the table in front of my chair. I looked down and sat with a blank stare, with glazed-over eyes as I absorbed the awkward silence that ensued after we all said hello.

"We thought we would celebrate your first commission check with some exciting opportunities. You have been doing a great job and we want to reward you for that and just protect you going forward. We would like to offer you 3% of the company."

"Wow! Really?"

"Yes. You just need to sign these papers and then I will give you your check, we can eat quickly, and then I know you want to get home to get some rest."

"Oh my gosh, thank you so much! I really appreciate this."

"And now that you are part business owner with us, we wanted to take out an insurance policy to protect you. It is a smart idea to do that when you own a business, so we went ahead and started that too."

At the time, 3% sounded like a whole lot compared to 0%. I was tired, hungry, and poor — this was a near-lethal combination. When I awoke the next morning, I had a foreboding sense in the pit of my stomach. Something didn't feel right. Once the morning haze cleared, my intuition was sitting like a fireball in my stomach, rolling around and sending spitfire up my throat. *WHAT HAD I DONE???*

I replayed the blurry memory in my head from the night before. I could picture Lonnic's ditzy voice and swindling tone. Her husband just sitting there quietly, acting as the accomplice. I didn't understand what I signed, and I was afraid to look at the papers. I started remembering some key words from dinner, which at the time sounded like a good idea but outside of delirium sounded like I had just signed my life away into someone else's hands — someone else who happened to be greedy and sneaky and self-serving.

I scanned the papers and emailed them over to an attorney to review them. I needed to hear the general terms, from an expert, to outline what my future would hold. The attorney started off by telling me that my boss's intentions were not looking out for me, but for them. He told me that I had signed a non-compete and non-disclosure agreement, a key person insurance policy, and a 3% ownership agreement.

"What does that mean?"

"Well, the non-compete is unenforceable, so I wouldn't worry about it, but it states that if you leave the company, you cannot work in the design industry for two years. These never stand up in court and they drafted this by themselves, not through an attorney. Not to mention, a non-compete needs five sets of parameters for it to really be effective, and this one does not. In addition to that, they've got a lot of incorrect terminology in here regarding their own corporate structure, which really keeps this from being enforceable."

"OK, thank god. So what do the other two papers I signed mean for me?"

"The key person insurance policy is not insurance for you; it is insurance for them. If anything were to happen to you, whether you were sick, injured, or died, your bosses would be able to collect the revenue you bring into their company. It basically insures lost wages."

"Wow. They made it sound like they were doing me a favor ... like they took out this insurance policy to protect *me.*"

"No, ma'am. This is like them admitting that you are bringing a big chunk of their revenue, so without you, they would be in trouble financially. The insurance policy on you protects them from going out of business."

"That is disgusting. OK, now what about the 3%? Do I really own 3% of the company, and when and how do I get paid for that?"

"Again, they wrote this agreement. This is not a legal paper you signed. I would not say you legally own *anything* until you sign papers drawn up by and witnessed by an attorney. Usually, companies pay dividends at the end of each year, so you would receive 3% of the profit after all of the company expenses are paid."

"That sounds like another horrible deal. What am I going to do with 3%? So do I ask them to get me official legal documents for the ownership percentage?"

"Yes, I wouldn't take this seriously until you sign a legal document. I would ask them to meet with their attorney and go through this together. I also recommend that you get it in the contract that there is opportunity for a percentage increase up to a certain percentage. You can negotiate with them on those terms."

I was 25, naïve, and desperate to succeed. And I had been taken advantage of. Then I remembered something. Before I had taken this job, I worked for a custom decorating company where I worked with the same installer for several years. His name was Jim. Jim taught me a lot about installations of custom soft goods, but he also passed on his wisdom about working with customers. There was one thing Jim said to me that I had never forgotten:

I was 25, naïve, and desperate to succeed. And I had been taken advantage of.

"If you meet a customer, and the hairs on the back of your neck stand up, find a way to not work with that customer. Do whatever you can to find a way out — whether it be that you are too busy to make their deadline or you give them an estimate that you know they won't accept."

Shortly after I started this job at the design shop, Jim came to visit me during a lunch break, and I introduced him to Lonnie and Will. We walked out the front door and took a left to get some slices of pizza.

Jim told me, "Danielle, watch out for him."

"Watch out for who?"

"For her husband. I don't trust him."

"Really? He is so nice to me. I think he is just hard of hearing, so he comes off as less friendly than he really is."

"Danielle, do you remember what I told you? The hairs on the back of my neck stood up when I shook his hand."

Round Two

For all those years,
the truth was hidden
under layers of deceit.
But I finally accepted that
as long as I knew it,
I could be at peace.

And now here we are for "round two,"
with the ones being chased
playing against the chaser.
As they play the same game I am used to —
the one I never wanted to play —
chasing down the truth
and wondering if we can face her.

The Four-Letter Word

It had been 8 years since I had seen or spoken to my family, with the exceptions of my sister and my cousin Kim. My sister was now out of high school and working at a daycare center. The children she worked with seemed to give her purpose, which kept her out of the partying scene. She told me she had hooked up with someone she met online, allowing him to pick her up, drive her back to his home an hour away, and one poor decision led to another. The fallout was significant, but it seemed she was OK now. I will never know what really happened. She had no college plans and was barely making enough money to get by, though she was happy working with children and I saw her trying to heal her past through redemption once again. I understood.

My sister wanted to move down to North Carolina to get away from The Lady and our brother. Rumor had it that our brother was addicted to just about every drug he could get his hands on now, and after he climbed the side of the house and broke in through her bedroom window while she was sleeping, she no longer felt safe living there. I would do anything to get her out of there, so I felt nothing but excitement about her coming to North Carolina. I would get to spend Easter with her — my first family holiday since I was 12 years old. The second her decision was made, I started making her an Easter basket. I would make a ham dinner, we would bake desserts together, and we would have a quiet, normal, family holiday. For the first time in a long time, I had something to look forward to.

For three weeks, I shared my bed with my sister. I exercised with her in my empty living room and I took her everywhere with me. I brought her to networking events and got her babysitting jobs through my professional networking circle. I had begun dating someone, so while my sister was in town, I sought out alone time by staying at my boyfriend's place and gave her the bed to herself.

As the weeks went by, my sister would complain that I was waking up too early. I would come home to check on her mid-day and she would still be sleeping. All she wanted to do was sleep. She was less motivated to go places with me or get a consistent job. Her car was towed for parking in the handicap spot in my apartment lot and she was pulled over for a speeding ticket for not wearing her seatbelt. That was enough for her to start complaining about how she much she hated North Carolina. She had the victim mentality and always had — whatever happened to her, it was *never* her fault.

The Friday night before Easter Sunday, I got home from work and noticed the apartment looked emptier than normal. I called my sister's name. There was no answer. I checked the counter for a note. There was no note. I opened the closet. Her items were missing. I looked in the bedroom and the bathroom. Nothing.

My sister was gone, without a warning and without a trace. I called my friend who she was supposed to be babysitting for that night and he told me she had left in the morning to move back home to Massachusetts. I was heartbroken. Out of all the things she had done to me, this was by far the harshest disappointment.

Striking Out

Things at work seemed to be going from bad to worse. Lonnie and Will were increasingly absent from the business and they shared that they were starting to doubt how profitable the business was. I crunched the numbers for my jobs and knew that the data was strong, but I did not take these accusations lightly. I called an emergency meeting with them, including their accountant and our assistant Melissa (whose hours dedicated to my projects I was now required to pay for, per Lonnie). I had all the responsibilities of a true independent contractor and business owner, without the power and the assurances about the future.

For the meeting, I had the table ready with five chairs. I requested the bank statements to be present at the meeting and Lonnie was making copies of them at the printer, causing a delay in the meeting's start time. Everyone was quiet and still. I demanded transparency so we could attempt to clear the air about the financial status of the company. As I opened the stapled pages of bank statements related to the business credit card account, Melissa and I quickly found whited-out lines. Right as I was about to question Lonnie, I started reading off all the non-business, frequent purchases listed directly below the redacted lines. There are many that I still remember clearly: Harris Teeter groceries, flip flops, flights to Puerto Rico, a $26,000 construction draw for a new home in Myrtle Beach. Why were these purchases being made on the business credit card — on the same business account for which the entire team was being scrutinized when it came to company profitability? My stomach sank the same way it did when I signed those papers. These people were crooks. The IRS just hadn't figured it out yet.

After the meeting, I also asked Lonnie if she had the legal document showing that I was 3% owner. She said that her attorney had been sick and then he was on vacation. It had been three months since our meeting at the country club. Nothing about the way they had tried to box me into a corner had been resolved to my benefit. My stomach sank again.

I kept working, hoping things would get better. Lucinda and Eugene — my friends and mentors who owned the successful painting business and who got me involved with K&M Networking — invited me on a little getaway. Together, we planned a trip to a historic fort from the Civil War called Brunswick Town. I was dating a guy named Anthony, who was a few years younger than me. We had met in the networking group and Anthony was an up-and-coming financial advisor who wore suits every day and who, at 25, owned his first home. He was in the same place as me with his career: he was young and he was hungry. But aside from that, we had nothing in common. Anthony agreed to join us on the trip, a sort of "double date."

When the day arrived for our trip to Brunswick Town, I was burned out in every way. I had only slept two hours after finishing a design project at 5:00 a.m. But tired as I was, I refused to cancel plans with my friends. We visited the ruins of the old colonial town, then the four of us went to lunch. The conversation geared toward business, our favorite topic. Then Lucinda started curating the moment that changed my life.

"So when are you going to go out on your own?"

"Well, I would love to, but I don't have the money for that."

Eugene got a pensive look on his face and asked, "So is money the only thing standing in your way?"

"Of course it is! Money is *always* the only thing standing in my way."

"How much does an interior design business need for start-up costs?"

"Probably between $40,000 and $50,000."

"Hmm."

There was a moment of silence before Lucinda picked up the conversation again.

"We feel that you are ready to be out on your own. Right now, your business partners are just using you as their cash cow. And we have watched you over the past year — we feel that you are ready. You should go out on your own."

"Really? Everyone keeps telling me that about Lonnie and Will. It is getting bad. They keep arguing over finances and, in May, they had me sign these sketchy papers, so I feel like I can't leave. Plus, it's not like I can go to a bank and get a loan and there aren't any firms here where I can make the money I am making now — especially now that I am making bonuses."

Eugene glanced at Lucinda and answered, "I believe that I am speaking for the both of us when I say that we are willing to loan you anywhere up to $50,000 for you to go out on your own. You are ready."

I can still see my face. I can feel the shock. It was an out-of-body experience, as my head started spinning, my vision blurred, and I began to black out my surroundings. I can see my shoulders folding inward as I broke out into an uncontrollable cry, trying to hide my face behind my napkin, as we sat in the middle of a restaurant. This was a different form of shock — a kind I had never experienced. For once, it wasn't about fear or terror, disappointment or despair. It was about something new and wonderful. Reacting to this kind of feeling was uncomfortable for me because I wasn't conditioned for these emotions — to the generosity that seemed completely overwhelming and to the love of true friends. No matter how hard we try, I think we all gravitate toward our comfort zones or patterns in vulnerable moments; the truth is that I was more comfortable getting beaten than being given money, faith, compassion, or love.

Maybe if I had gotten more sleep that previous night, I would have been able to form a sentence sooner, but my entire body broke out into emotion, where I blotted my eyes, wiped my nose, and tried to put out at least a stutter.

"Are you serious?"

They both nodded while looking me straight in the eyes with a simultaneous "*yes.*"

"Are you crazy? I don't have anything. I don't have any collateral. I live in an empty apartment. The only thing I own is a dog and I'm in tons of student loan debt."

"We know you are ready, and we trust you to pay us back. The offer remains open so you can think about it and let us know at any point in time if this is something you want to do."

"I could never borrow money like that from you. I couldn't live with myself."

"We know you will pay us back. We aren't worried about that part."

Anthony and I left the restaurant and I remained stiff, in complete disbelief that two people I had known for a little over a year (who I met in a McDonald's parking lot, in a minivan!) had just offered to loan me the amount of money that I was just now making in an entire year. I was just a hopeful, young professional trying to be a successful interior designer ... who had nothing but passion in my pockets and a strong work ethic on my resume. I thought about how crazy they were, while at the same time wondering how I was so lucky to meet two people who seemed to believe in me more than I believed in myself ... and more than anyone else in my life ever had.

 I thought about how crazy they were, while at the same time wondering how I was so lucky to meet two people who seemed to believe in me more than I believed in myself ... and more than anyone else in my life ever had.

After returning from our day-trip to a town that was now "historic" to me for very personal reasons, I walked in the door to my empty, ground-floor apartment that smelled like basement mildew. I had recently moved across town and had to sell my sofa to help pay for the move. I was now living just outside the train tracks in an area where that phrase "they live on the other side of the tracks" must have been coined. When you turned left of the tracks, you ended up in a beautiful neighborhood called Forest Hills, where the trees were overhanging the streets. But if you turned to the right of the tracks, you ended up in a part of town where you were apt to hear gunshots, see drug deals, and pick up rumors and signs of gang activity. I turned on the light switch in my new home on the not-so-idyllic side of town and the cockroaches ran back behind the fridge. I tried to forget they were there, but I slept with my door shut so they couldn't sneak into my bed. I only kept food inside the fridge because I knew that if I left anything unsecured, the pests would take over and I would no longer have a place to live.

Out of instinct and seeking for comfort, I went to the fridge to look for something to eat. I saw my list of passions on the door and I closed the fridge, staring and breathing slowly and deliberately. I did a double take over that "passion card" about owning my own interior design business. OH MY GOD, THIS REALLY WORKS. I had manifested my dream, with the help of some truly amazing and generous people.

I took the paper out from under the magnet and sat on the living room carpet. I pretended this was my yoga and exercising room. I laid down, staring at the ceiling, glancing at the list, then staring at the ceiling, glancing at the list ...

Cooper laid against my side and licked my nose until I got up and grabbed another piece of yellow-lined paper. I drew a horizontal line and a vertical line crossing over it, about halfway on the page. On the left side I wrote PROS and on the right side I wrote CONS. It was time to seriously consider the idea of becoming an entrepreneur.

I spent a week mulling over the list, making sure I did not miss any make-it-or-break-it selling points. This list meant nothing yet; but, to me, it meant hope. In that moment, I felt different. I felt like I would have a successful future, a living room with a sofa, and a backyard for Cooper. I didn't feel trapped anymore. I had a way out of this job with these bosses who were taking advantage of me and I didn't have to feel sick to my stomach anymore. On my list, I had a full column of bullet points on the PROS side, but on the CONS side, there was only one word: FEAR.

 In that moment, I felt different. I felt like I would have a successful future, a living room with a sofa, and a backyard for Cooper. I didn't feel trapped anymore.

I called Lucinda and Eugene to set up a meeting for Saturday night to discuss the details of the loan they were offering. I realized how stupid I would be to pass up an opportunity like this because of fear — that four-letter word I hated to say and had spent enough of my life feeling. Fear had dominated the first 18 years of my life. Why would I embrace and accept the word I hated the most? I hated what this word meant and what it did to me. It does not deserve to take anything else from me — whether it's happiness, family, or opportunities.

I never owed money to anyone, nevermind to two people I cared about, and I knew I would not let myself fail. Fear was just an illusion and failure wasn't an option, because I would not let it be. I knew myself well enough and believed in myself enough to know this.

When I showed up at Lucinda and Eugene's house, we started to discuss details over pepperoni pizza. Then they wanted to watch a movie called *The Secret*, which was the movie I read about while reading *The Passion Test*. We agreed to 10% interest plus 15% of the profit on client orders for a 5-year loan term.

The next morning, the name of my future company came to me while I was in the shower: Port City Design Group. Shower thoughts are real. The hotter the water is, the more I feel like Einstein. After my shower, I sat down at my computer and made my logo. I emailed Lonnie about scheduling a meeting Friday afternoon with her and Will. *I will see you both at 2:00 p.m.* I was going to do this with integrity, and I refused to work for anyone while being mentally checked out, so I wanted to have this conversation as quickly as possible.

Thursday, October 2, 2014

I was handed a check for $40,000 to start my company. I was so nervous to be holding that much money, so I went straight to the bank and deposited it. Seeing my bank account with this many zeros gave me this flickering Christmas-light moment combined with a hand-wavering HOLY SHIT.

Once the check was in the bank, I called a co-working office space called CoWorx and rented a small 350-square-foot office, which included a desk, two office chairs and an office phone, and access to a communal bathroom and a shared conference room.

Friday, October 3, 2014

I walked into the store and it was just Lonnie. I asked when Will would be arriving, and she mentioned that he was playing golf that day. I walked up to my office and grabbed my personal items off the desk. They did not understand how important this meeting was.

As Lonnie was in the store by herself, I asked her how we could have an uninterrupted meeting, knowing that a customer could come walking in. She said she would lock the door during the time of our meeting so that we wouldn't be interrupted.

I told Lonnie that I appreciated the opportunity to work for her and Will, and that I was grateful for my time with them. I explained that an unexpected opportunity presented itself and that I was being loaned money to start my own company and that I would be stupid to pass up the offer. I promised her that she was the first to know of my decision, and that I wanted to give her a final two weeks' notice but I knew it would have been a conflict of interest to keep working for her while I was seeking to build my own client base for Port City Design Group. Because I was a 1099 independent contractor, I didn't really need to "give notice" at all, but I had been working — for all intents and purposes — as an employee. The lines were quite blurred, but I did what I felt was right. I was paid once a month and we were just three days into the month of October so I offered to forego payment for the last three days of work. I handed over all billable hours for my clients so she could send out invoices. I left by saying that I wanted to continue to work together and pass referrals back and forth. I had tears in my eyes and I gave Lonnie a hug, walking out on a meeting that I felt could not have gone better.

I contacted Melissa and let her know that I had left the company. I knew she would, in all likelihood, no longer have a job (because she primarily supported my work at the shop and now I was gone), so I offered her the opportunity to work for me as my office manager — but only after she spoke to Lonnie the next day. Together, we went to Staples and HomeGoods, getting everything we needed to open our doors on Monday.

That night at 8:30 p.m., I received an email from Lonnie. She demanded that I provide information about my investors, as she was going to take legal action against each of us. She asked for my tablet back, which was a Christmas present she had given to me 10 months prior. I decided not to answer the message, as I assumed the email came from her post-shock emotions (with Will's input) and that her anger would soon disappear.

Saturday, October 4, 2014

I had Melissa drop off the tablet when she handed in her resignation. Lonnie told Melissa that if she worked for me or had any affiliation with me, that she would drag her into the lawsuit she was going to file against me.

I emailed my clients with a vague and professional email, letting them know that I was given an amazing opportunity to start my own firm. I left it open-ended so the clients felt comfortable coming to me to continue working with them, but I made sure they wouldn't feel solicited. I began hearing from them shortly thereafter, once each of them received a phone call from Lonnie, during which Lonnie said that I was not allowed to steal her company's clients and that they should refrain from having a working relationship with me.

Monday, October 6, 2014

I was officially an entrepreneur! I owned an interior design firm, Port City Design Group, which was up and running with 1 employee, 1 computer, 350 square feet, and 0 clients.

Thursday, October 9, 2014

I was about to attend my first K&M Networking meeting as the owner of Port City Design Group. I was so excited to share my news with my favor-

First office space on the first day of business as the owner of Port City Design Group, October 6, 2014.

ite group of people in town. I curled my hair and I wore a form-fitting navy dress with teal earrings to match my company colors.

There were approximately 60 of us in the room that day. I am claustrophobic and sat at one of the three tables up against the front wall instead of sinking myself into the crowd in the middle of the room. My back was facing the door when I felt this unnerving sense that everyone was looking at me. I turned to see Lonnie and Will entering the room, with their intentions written all over their faces.

I faced back toward the wall and heard Will slide his chair out right behind mine. Then I felt his chair, sliding into the back of my chair, so that I couldn't get out, as my rib cage pressed against the edge of the table.

Lonnie stood up first, for her 60-second elevator speech. As awkward as they wanted it to be, I wasn't going to let them take away my excitement about my big announcement. I left their company on good terms and I was going to keep it that way. I pushed my chair back into Will's with clear struggle and I got out from under the table and walked to the front of the room, announcing the birth of Port City Design Group. The praise and clapping was contagious.

As I sat back down in my chair, Will turned his head and loudly whispered, "Not for long, Danielle. You better watch out."

I turned my head back around to face the wall, while I could see that the first few rows of members had heard what he said. The members notified the director and that was the last time they attended a meeting.

October 20, 2014 — My 26th Birthday

Melissa and I were in the office when I received a phone call, which read on my caller ID as the local sheriff's department.

"Hello?"

A friendly and firm female voice jumped in, "Yes ma'am ... this is Officer Landley. Is this Miss Boisse?"

"This is she."

"Miss Boisse, I am confirming your location at 2512 Independence Road."

"Yes, ma'am. May I ask what this call is about?"

"Ms. Boisse, you are being served and we ask that you remain in your location while the sheriff makes his way to you in the next half hour."

"What do you mean, served? What does that mean?"

"You have been served with a lawsuit, ma'am. You will receive all the paperwork from the sheriff, who is on his way to you now."

"Officer, who is the lawsuit from?"

"Exemplify Design."*

---

* "Exemplify Design" is a pseudonym. Out of respect and confidentiality, the actual plaintiff organization's name is being withheld from this book.

"Oh, wow. Can you tell me what the lawsuit is regarding?"

"I cannot, but there are actually three lawsuits here. One for you personally, one for Melissa Garcia, and one for Port City Design Group."

"WOW. I don't know what is happening right now, but I really need you to call the sheriff and tell him he cannot come in this office building. I work around a dozen other companies in a co-working space and I CANNOT have him serve me in a public space like this. I will leave my office right now and come pick up the paperwork myself. PLEASE. Do not let him come here."

"OK, I will try to call him right now and see if he can turn around and I will call you to confirm."

I showed up at the sheriff's office and received my second stack of papers from my previous employer. This stack was my 26th birthday present.

Part 3
180 DEGREES

Even when you are still breaking the chains — with each link representing one more step towards a new life — the ability to start over is where the truest form of freedom lies. Starting over is a gift, a gift better than any missed birthday or Christmas disappointment.

I was not always on the right side of luck and, of course, there would be challenges in this new world, but there was no battle I would face without confidence, because nothing was as bad as the black hole I left. I felt like I could conquer anything.

I was in the light now, but the darkness was still trying to follow me. I needed to relearn the temptation, recognize it, face it, and stand up for who I was in the light.

I was creating my world — with a career I had passion for and my humble apartment. I was expanding and creating my family.

I was in the light of the sun, seeing myself for the first time. I was going to be someone. I was designing my life, the same way I had painted it in my head for 26 years.

New Life

A push and pull of struggle and luck,
my life forces me to look around
to understand the purpose,
through reflection,
off this chaotic crowd
and of the deafening noise
that sometimes overwhelms me.
I seek silence
over suffering —
embracing the bad silences
for the lessons they offer,
and the good silences for progression.
Both types of pauses
have changed my course and my pace,
pushed me further,
so I could make it here ...
to this new life, and to you.

Keep the Lights On

I held my face above the sink as the water poured from the faucet and onto my swollen eyes. My screams were everywhere — spiraling down the drain and rebounding off the walls, pounding and throbbing back at me. Mucus dripped from my nose like strings of yarn and, each time I screamed, more threads dropped into the basin of the sink, as the echoes sprang across the room and boomeranged back to me, "*WHYYYY? WHYYYYYYY!*"

Lonnie had placed a "stop payment" order on my last paycheck and on Melissa's last paycheck. She told her bank they were fraudulent deposits. I was only paid once a month, so that amount of money unexpectedly being taken out of my bank account was a significant hit. Every day, it was something new. It felt like I was being repeatedly stabbed in the same wound.

I had to hire an attorney to defend us. Melissa and I parallel-parked on 3rd Street downtown and walked into the Bank of America Building, taking the elevator to the top floor. This was one of the tallest, most corporate-looking buildings downtown and although the view was impressive, the lobby felt expensive and the air was stiff. It felt like this was a place for people who did bad things and who needed to weasel their way out. I didn't feel like we belonged here.

Lonnie and Will hired two attorneys to represent them, so we had to match their ammo. Benton and Patrick were younger attorneys who specialized in employment law and business litigation. Melissa and I shared our experience working for Exemplify Design and I handed them the paperwork they had me sign in May, just five months ago. I explained exactly what happened during the transition — of how I decided to stop contracting for Exemplify and establish my own firm, Port City Design Group. I told them that I had an attorney review the documents I had signed back in the early summer, and that I was advised that non-competes are very hard to enforce and wouldn't hold up in court, and that I didn't legally own 3% of the company, despite what Lonnie and Will promised. Benton shared that in North Carolina, if you verbally agree or shake hands over an agreement, it is considered a legal agreement. I had no idea. Different lawyers, different advice. This was getting so complicated.

Benton and Patrick listened, offered some scenarios, and handed me an affidavit that I needed my four clients to sign, stating that I did not solicit them to follow me to my new company. Then they explained what a retainer was; without me paying a retainer for their legal services, they would not start working on the case. Legal retainers were much different from orthodontist retainers, which was the only background I had on the subject. They meant money, and I mean serious money. The first retainer that was due up front, was SEVEN THOUSAND FIVE HUNDRED DOLLARS. I had never written a check for this much money before. I was so overwhelmed.

I was already in the red financially and in the dark emotionally, and this was just the first step of this legal battle. I had no idea how serious this was. My mind was panicking: *I am going to lose everything. Wait a second, I don't have anything. I owe people money. I must get through this in order to pay them back.* The $7,500 retainer did not include our awaited day in court. Then we would be billed for each email and phone call — every six minutes at rates that translated to $250 an hour. I had to go back to Lucinda and Eugene for an additional $5,000 loan because the startup loan they gave me was already used on opening accounts with vendors, opening orders, and purchasing a computer and office supplies. Two weeks in business and I was already in the red.

Once hired, Benton and Patrick were working on our case and, in the meantime, Melissa and I resumed business as usual. I was networking every day and put my focus on my clients and strengthening relationships with builders and subcontractors. The days were long, and I found a way to cover up my anxiety and anger. I went on a serious work binge. I woke up early and went to bed late. The fear of being homeless had started to flare, so I kept myself unhealthfully busy to suppress all other thoughts from creeping into my head. My focus on making it out of this was sharper than a machete.

 Two weeks in business and I was already in the red.

I left the office one Saturday morning and came home to discover a plumbing catastrophe in the bathroom, which had flooded my entire apartment. There was already black mold growing on and in the bathroom walls and my carpets were soaked with brown, putrid toilet water. The maintenance manager called the community manger, and he deemed my apartment a total loss. He offered me two options: I could either move out for a month and not pay rent until they could get me back into a unit, or he would let me out of my lease without a penalty, refund me one month's rent, and I could be on my way. I didn't have any money or a place to live temporarily or permanently, so I took the refunded rent, packed my clothes into three organized trash bags, and set up my $10 yard-sale desk at my boyfriend's house. He lived in a small two-bedroom house with a roommate and, as I learned all too quickly, he was not ready to live together. I was only able to spend a few nights there and then I needed to take my trash bags somewhere else. I was homeless, *again*. I take that back; it was Cooper *and* me. My little pup and best friend was in this with me. *We* were homeless.

Eat, Work, Sleep — Living to Work and Living at Work

My office was in a co-working space with many start-up companies, so everyone was hustling, hungry, and working late. My office door had a window on it, so I would work later than the last person in the office, and once I knew everyone had left the building, Cooper and I would sleep on the floor. I had a 4 x 6 area rug that gave us some cushion and I would bring one blanket inside. This is where I learned how to sleep without a pillow.

My hairdresser, Laura, who was one of my friends from K&M Speed Networking, let us stay in her bonus room for several weeks. The bonus room had its own back entrance. Laura had two young children and two large dogs, so I tried to stay at work as long as possible, so that we left before they woke up and got home after they were asleep. The bonus room had a sofa and a bed. When we would get home, I would set my laptop on my lap and then I would sleep there with Cooper on my stomach. I could not bring myself to sleep on the bed because of the guilt I felt for staying there. No matter how welcoming Laura's family was, I could not help feeling like a nuisance. I didn't like having to ask for favors and I didn't like that I was living a secret life — business owner during the day and homeless at night. Throughout my childhood and even through college, my friends would take me in as the orphan on holidays and vacations. I always felt uncomfortable for costing them money and, as much as I needed a place to go, I just wanted to be invisible while I was there. Accepting the hospitality of others has always been difficult for me.

Each morning, I was grabbing my clothes out of trash bags inside my trunk. My trash bags were organized as follows:

Bag 1: Work clothes

Bag 2: Pajamas, sweatpants, and sweatshirts.

Bag 3: Shoes and gym clothes.

I would stay at Anthony's house on most weekend nights and do my laundry there, so I wasn't using the water and electricity at Laura's house.

The Lawsuit Rolls On

Benton, one of the two lawyers representing me and Melissa as we fought the Exemplify lawsuit, had warned me about getting a letter in the mail for a preliminary motion. He told me that if I received this to call him immediately. The day came, and my legal lessons were now filling space in my hippocampus. Lonnie and Will wanted our case to be reviewed without delaying an action against me, as most lawsuits took at least a year to be seen in court. Benton said their intention was to put me out of business effective immediately, and this was one possible way to do that. Melissa and I went back downtown to prepare our case with Benton and Patrick.

November 4th was our day in court, and Melissa and I could not find our way to the court room; we were momentarily lost as we joked that we didn't belong here. The courthouse was a maze of echoing concrete walls and we felt so small within its cold architecture. We did not want to be there, obviously, but we really did not want to see Lonnie and Will either. We got off the elevator and there they were, whispering back and forth with their accountant, the same accountant who had sat at the table with me and Melissa the day we reviewed the redacted credit card statements and saw the writing on the wall. That accountant, she knew the truth, yet there she was — dragged into the case against her own will, because she would rather be an ally than an enemy. I, on the other hand, chose integrity —the "hard right" instead of the "easy wrong." I would rather be the enemy, even if it took everything I had, because I knew right from wrong and I now knew how much I had been taken advantage of. Enough. Being the victim was part of my old life, not my new one. I was never willingly accepting that role again.

We sat down in the sterile court room with gray walls, gray chairs, and gray carpets; I stared at the broken fluorescent lighting dangling above our heads. The room was cold and the tension shifted our energy as we walked through the door. The judge was an elderly man who looked like a sweet grandpa to a bunch of grandkids. He seemed like he had a heart, so I was hopeful that he would see this for what it was. I hoped he would see the two little girls on the right side of the court room and know that we were innocent. I was not anyone important — like a doctor, a dentist, or a lawyer. I was a 26-year-old interior designer, for crying out loud! There are so many people who don't want to work and all I want to do is work! LEAVE ME ALONE AND LET ME GO HOME. Well, let me go back to my homeless home. It was just starting, and I already felt defeated.

The opposing attorney was the longest practicing attorney in the county. I believe it was 57 years that year. His co-counsel added some youth and novice to the table. I was observing every move that was being made by all parties in the room, trying to gauge the temperature.

We were shivering in our seats, and I could not tell if it was the temperature or nerves. The opposing side approached Benton and Patrick. They walked to the back of the court room and, after a quick discussion, they notified us of their offering. They knew this case would not stand in court, so they offered a $10,000 settlement to drop the case that day. That would be $340,000 less than the suit initially demanded. My response went something like this, "My answer is *no*. I am not paying them a penny."

Benton and Patrick thought this was a fair deal because ending this nonsense — for $10,000 — would keep me from paying them the $10,000 in legal fees if we ended it here.

"I would rather pay *you* than pay them," I explained. "Paying them is like admitting I did something wrong. I am not going to pay them $350,000 or $10,000."

Although no one who knows me would be surprised by my stubborn response, even I could recognize that, in this situation, I had to walk a fine line between being stubborn and being poor. But this was like playing poker. I thought I could call their bluff and have them drop everything. They were paying their attorneys a significant amount more than I was paying mine, and because they were clearly motivated by money, I couldn't imagine they wanted to keep spending on lawsuits what they could be frittering away on groceries, flip flops, Puerto Rican vacations, or their holiday home in Myrtle Beach.

The back and forth continued with the attorneys, which seemed like a complete waste of time and money. They started giving us worse offers than their first offer. They thought they had gained leverage when, in fact, they had lost me on their first crappy offer. They were now asking for a percentage of my profits in the company I was just getting off the ground! I was not going to make any ridiculous compromises, so we went in front of the judge.

The opposing attorney started his case. He described me as a malicious monster. He said I had locked Lonnie in a bathroom, stole her business key to the front door, and threatened to steal her clients and leave the company. I thought I had faced the biggest liars of my life during my childhood but apparently they were everywhere — including the court room, where it was illegal to lie under oath. My face filled with fury as I aggressively started scribbling on my piece of paper, passing notes to my attorneys. We were warned that Lonnie and Will's attorney would employ tactics that would be aggressive, but I never anticipated this sort of strategy — attacking me personally and spinning falsehoods about my words and behaviors. As I watched his theatrical performance, I felt their beady eyes staring at me across the room. I hated all of them.

Melissa and I never took the stand. Benton said we didn't need to. Luckily, Lonnie's statements on the stand did more damage than we could have asked for. We had evidence against her — between repetitive behavior with previous employees and illegal behavior defined by the Department of Labor. We left the courtroom that day with a continuance and without a resolution.

It Has to Get Worse Before It Gets Better

It was time to find a more permanent, though semi-permanent place to live. Per my promise to Laura, my stay there was temporary. But "home sweet home" was elusive. I didn't even have $500 in my bank account while our day in court cost another $3,500. This meant I couldn't get an apartment just yet, because that would require two months' rent up front and a $250 pet fee. The money simply wasn't there. I had that uncomfortable and embarrassed stomach-sinking feeling as I scrolled through my phone's contact records and made a list of people who might have an extra room for me (in addition to allowing a small dog). I stopped at the letter A to write down the first name as I thought about my friend Anna, who was a thriving single mom with two teenage girls and a dog. I asked Anna if I could stay the month in her spare bedroom for $400. She agreed. Here I was sharing and cleaning a bathroom with two teenage girls and I could not have been more grateful.

I was on autopilot — faking it more than I ever had before. I kept the lawsuit a secret from almost everyone. I was embarrassed by it. I did not want anyone to know that my business could be in danger of collapse. So I continued smiling and working and exuding optimism and confidence at every turn. I showed up every day acting like I owned a successful company. If you didn't know better, you'd have guessed I lived in a house with a white picket fence and shopped for designer purses on the weekends. I hated being fake and I never was a good actress, but if I didn't protect the truth, my reputation as a new business owner would never make it. There was too much at stake, and my ego was the least of it. I needed food and shelter.

Meanwhile, the legal posturing continued. It seemed like the offers from the opposing side were getting more and more out of touch with reality, which meant our phone calls from Benton were getting more and more stressful. Then came one phone call I will never forget — a conversation that triggered in me the biggest state of paralyzing shock I have ever experienced ... the kind where time stops, where your heart stops, where everything goes black. It had been a long time since an abuser had thrown me down a flight of stairs or jumped on my stomach, but this felt surprisingly similar.

The sky was dark too early now, and all the offices were empty and cold from the draft whispering through the windows. It was a Thursday evening. Benton and Patrick were both on the line. I knew it was serious.

Benton spoke first, "We received the judge's verdict this evening, and the judge didn't rule the motion in our favor."

"OK, what do you mean?"

"We were notified that you will need to stop seeing clients until we appear again in court."

I choked on my saliva. This was the first and only time in my life where I wanted to speak, and I couldn't. I pictured my dad at the McDonald's drive-through, trying to order our chicken nuggets and unable to speak. Nothing was coming out of my mouth.

The silence lingered and it felt like the entire world had stopped spinning. My eyes were blurry, and my throat and lungs were burning.

"Wh-wha-what do you mean I can't see clients?"

"From what we were told, you will need to close down Port City Design Group until we are seen in court."

"What am I supposed to do, Benton? I need to work. I owe people money and I have bills to pay!"

"I know. I was not expecting this. I am going to call the judge and ask for clarification, but I am not sure when I will hear back. This is all I know from the phone call we had."

"So, I need to go get another job until the lawsuit is seen in court?"

"Yes, but as the motion states, you cannot operate as a competing business."

"What if I do design at Home Depot?"

"No ..."

"No? I can't work at Home Depot?"

"You can't work in the design field at all."

I cried out what seemed to be every ounce of moisture in my body. The forceful screaming and crying caused my body to jerk back and forth, which left my back in painful agony. I tried to ice my swollen eyelids, but it still hurt to blink and it looked like I had been struck in the face with a sledgehammer. I was a young woman who had escaped physical abuse only to now find herself looking in the mirror to see someone who looked every part the "battered woman." I felt ugly and sad, broken and attacked. Not being able to put on a brave face — or at least one that wasn't swollen — wasn't helping my morale.

As I sat alone with the news of this latest blow, I found myself remembering moments of emotional despair when I was a child. I recall being in the 6th grade and receiving my first C on a report card. It was actually a C+ and it was in math. To me, my struggle with learning math versus my other subjects didn't seem reasonable. It didn't seem fair. I was a straight-A student with OCD who needed to get straight A's for myself — not because anyone was looking at my report cards or grounding me if I got a C, but because how I felt about myself was all I had in this world. My perfectionism was an illness that was becoming paralyzing. I received my report card on a Friday and when I went home, I locked myself in my room until Monday morning. I came out not because I wanted to go back to school but because, in my mind, I needed to have perfect attendance; I could not miss a day and make something *else* imperfect. I stared at the C+ in shock, hundreds of times, crying and grieving my own life, because I thought my life was over, and I was a failure. I was too embarrassed to tell my best friend, Liesl, who was smart and would never get a C+. I did not answer the phone and my friends kept calling, wondering if I was alive. I felt deep pain that weekend and I considered whether life was worth living because really, *my life was over, everything was over.* It's a story that may sound melodramatic to a healthy adult, but my despair in that moment, wrapped in the kind of childhood I was living, was real. And it was dangerous. Now, some 14 years later, I was told I couldn't work or earn a living — that my life was being put on pause and that my value to my clients or to the world was irrelevant. I was despondent beyond measure. I felt like that 6th grader all over again.

The next morning, after having cried all night about Benton and Patrick's phone call, I felt empty inside. My purpose was gone. I didn't know what to do or where to go, so I went into the office, regardless of what we were told last night. Until Benton clarified the situation with the judge, I was going to keep working, but in silence.

I called Eugene and told him I had to talk. I told him it was bad, and we should meet in person. He drove to town and met me in my office parking lot. Eugene was 43 at this point — clean cut with blonde-gray gelled hair that matched his fair complexion. He wore glasses that made him look like the perfect candidate to dress as Santa Claus during the holiday season. With his wife Lucinda, Eugene had owned Coastal Painting and Improvements for almost 10 years at this point and they had gone through the peaks and valleys of having it all and losing it all. They decided to keep living, in some ways, like they *had* lost it all, which left Eugene driving an old truck that didn't go in reverse. Both dangerous and ridiculous, Eugene pulled into a parking spot that he wouldn't need to reverse out of.

I looked at him and couldn't talk without crying — first for the guilt I felt for letting them be dragged into the mud with me by virtue of the favor they had given me, then for the embarrassment of him seeing me like this, and lastly for the fact that I owed him and his wife $45,000 and I was being told that I was no longer allowed to work in my field. I was willing to work anywhere or everywhere, but I know I couldn't pay my bills working at McDonald's. What the hell was I going to do now??

Eugene listened and stayed calm. I saw the fear in his face, even though he had a better poker face than me. Then he looked at me and said, "Danielle, I don't care what they tell you. Listen to me: you go back into your office and keep serving your clients. Keep making phone calls, keep selling jobs, and keep your lights on. You are *going* to keep your lights on."

I took a deep breath and took his advice. I walked back into my office and flipped the light switch. I was going to remain open until confirmation from the judge told me otherwise. I thought about what Eugene had said. It wasn't only the literal meaning of "keeping the lights on" that I needed to hear — it was the metaphorical meaning too. When times got tough, I didn't throw in the towel and turn off the lights, I kept shining my light and pushed through the darkness. I couldn't give up on Lucinda and Eugene for loaning me the money, I couldn't give up on Melissa who was relying on me for income, I couldn't give up on my clients, and I couldn't give up on myself. I didn't stop fighting for the truth when I was a kid, and I wasn't going to stop now. I was born to fight, work, build, and succeed.

No More Holidays

As resigned as I was to keep pushing forward, I was emotionally exhausted. And it was taking a toll on my body as well. I had completely lost my appetite. My thoughts and vision were dim and hazy. My eyes were so heavy and small. In my mind, as I waited for news about a second (and hopefully final) day in court, I replayed that first experience with all the lawyers and the judge. I saw Lonnie and Will — each of their faces staring at me across the court room, wishing for me to give up and go out of business, wanting me to hurt, fail and lose. I kept trying to understand, but there was no answer, except for greed. I couldn't let someone else's greed take me down.

Benton called. He had personally spoken with the judge over the phone. The judge was puzzled as to how or why the inaccuracies had been communicated to us, but nevertheless, the news we had heard yesterday was *not* true. I could keep working — in my industry and in my new company. The judge urged us to try and make an agreement with the plaintiff's attorneys outside of court while reiterating that the only ones who win in court are the attorneys. With this huge sigh of relief, life seemed livable again — after the 24-hour rollercoaster that had given me a ride that was anything but fun. In this lawsuit, the other side was not like us. They were using tactics that seemed heartless and cruel, selfish and petty, vindictive and arrogant. Now, thanks to them, I had less trust for people and their intentions, as I realized that evil also existed outside of Birchcroft Road — that adults were sometimes awful to adults, and not just their children.

As the stress of money (or, more accurately, not enough of it) grew, I was increasingly adamant about getting a second job. But if I was going to start moonlighting, I wanted to play it undercover because it was important to me that no one know that money was tight and I was hustling to make ends meet. Anthony had a friend who worked at a Christmas-tree lot that was set up outside a gas station on the north side of town. I begged my way in and they gave me a job that seemed pretty enjoyable. I would be using the scraps of pine that had been cut off the trees to press into a metal ring and make Christmas wreaths, in three different sizes. Here was the best part — they would pay me cash. They offered me $3 for small, $5 for medium, and $8 for the large wreaths.

Here I was, covering my face as much as I could with my hair and a winter hat, with freezing feet and hands, covered in sap, hiding in the back of a Christmas tree lot beside a gas station. I was 26 with a bachelor's degree and a small business that was successful enough to keep up with the legal bills in its first two months of business. My fear of being "found out" escalated when I heard a familiar voice coming around the corner. It was Angie, a woman from K&M. She noticed me. I had to think quickly, since she had been seeing me at networking meetings, dressed in dresses and heels, advertising my new high-end interior design firm. I told Angela I was volunteering here, making wreaths (when, in fact, I was working for grocery money). At the time, being there and being noticed made me hate Lonnie and Will even more.

The fall and winter had historically brought me pain and disappointment. I was trapped in the house with my dysfunctional family when New England winters arrived, and the "highlights" of the season were never highlights for me. I never liked my birthday and I hated Christmas. As was the case with The Lady, Lonnie also managed to turn celebratory days into difficult memories — serving me with a lawsuit on my birthday and taking me to my knees financially for Christmas. While I crafted holiday wreaths with my cold hands, I remembered how The Lady always found a way to ruin my birthdays and Christmases — whether it was by making me invisible or deciding to make me *too* visible so she could pull out her most damaging behavior.

Before I stopped celebrating birthdays and holidays with my family (when I was 12), The Lady would buy me the exact things I told her I didn't want. She ignored my wish lists and wouldn't even concede to my requests for gift cards instead of disappointment.

On my 12th Christmas, I tried to be a step ahead of the disappointment. It was maybe a week or two before Christmas. It was a Saturday. Liesl and I were home alone while The Lady was out with my sister and brother. I have no memory of where my dad was or whether perhaps he was immobile in a wheelchair at the time. There were a few presents under the tree and we collected all the wrapped gifts with my name on them. Of course, we didn't want to get caught, so we ingeniously discovered that a butter knife could disguise the opening of the tape and then be retaped without leaving any evidence.

We cut open one end of each gift, shocked by the number of turtlenecks that were purchased. Knit, thin, and thick — every wrapped turtleneck seemed like some sick joke, considering I had repeatedly told The Lady how much I hated turtlenecks. They were not cool for middle school, and they were not the $50 Gap fleece I really wanted; that one item I would have worn every day until next year when I would get another color. Liesl and I removed each turtleneck from each box, stuffed t-shirts in their place, and then made a trip to the mall to exchange each one for something else. On Christmas morning, I never came downstairs until everyone went to sleep, and I snuck my wrapped t-shirts back into my room. It was a small, but important, victory.

Now, as I was working to build a new life and a new identity for myself, those winter holiday disappointments loomed large. My 26th birthday and subsequent Christmas brought me something much worse than those turtlenecks and much more expensive than a Gap fleece hoodie. Thankfully, when New Year's Eve came, we received a letter that Lonnie and Will were dropping the lawsuit for a settlement of $5,000 with no other requests or strings attached. I saw this as a win. I'd write one more check to end this all, would avoid accruing additional legal fees, and would move on with my life and my business. As I saw it, they finally surrendered (though they inflicted a bit more pain) and the war was over, just in time for a new year. Benton called to congratulate me for my perseverance and grit, and laughed that he ought to take me with him to negotiate his next major purchase. I smiled.

My patience and tolerance for pretty much everything had worn pretty thin that year. My relationship with Anthony had ended and I was ready for a new year, leaving all the baggage behind in 2014. I felt like I had just made it through the three months of war, and now I was feeling on top of the world.

The Wall

As I gauge stability from a straight line,
these diagrams hurt my diaphragm,
and I still have trouble breathing.

My walls were poured from concrete,
reinforced and stable,
bending, but never breaking
or springing a leak.

Vulnerability exposes weakness
so I will stay in and hide …
safety first.
You can't see me;
my door is closed
while the jams are about to burst.

But you — only you — saw the cracks,
with light pouring through,
waiting to be shared and seen.

You saw the wall,
gently knocking it down,
as I feel everything now …
for the first time …
as my lungs take their deepest breaths.

12

Connecting the Dots

In 2015, I was the poster child for the motto "New Year, New You." I felt lighter as I shed another heavy layer of my past and as I continued the chase toward my ideal future. I was a dream chaser and a no-time-waster. By March, I had paid off my final bill for legal fees. Between the $5,000 to Exemplify Design and the law firm's fees, I was all in for $23,000. I paid it off in less than six months while still making interest and commission payments to Eugene and Lucinda. This was a major hit for any business, never mind for a new business; the money disappeared sometimes more quickly than it arrived, no matter how hard we worked. But as soon as I handed over the last check to my attorney, I looked at Port City Design Group and knew we had done it — my small but mighty company had climbed the mountain.

 I felt lighter as I shed another heavy layer of my past and as I continued the chase toward my ideal future. I was a dream chaser and a no-time-waster.

As it turned out, being homeless and desperate worked in my favor. It was as if I were being chased by a shark and if I stopped swimming, I would have been killed. "Sink or swim" is a common scenario we find ourselves in, and — in this case — I swam. I swam furiously to the piece of wood floating in the middle of the ocean, and I could barely breathe or feel my feet that were still dangling in the freezing water, but I was alive. I had a few more bruises on me, but a lot more wisdom. I had made it. I didn't sink.

Surviving 2014 and early 2015 left me with a fire in my belly that drove me. In time, the fire became a burning obsession — I was done being poor and homeless, I was done being naïve, I was done losing everything. I wanted the kind of life that I had always dreamed of … and I was willing to work for it. Nothing was going to stop me now.

I was done being poor and homeless, I was done being naïve, I was done losing everything. I wanted the kind of life that I had always dreamed of … and I was willing to work for it. Nothing was going to stop me now.

Better Times, In Every Way

I had a full schedule and was often working with up to 10 clients at a time now. I hired my first designer and we quickly outgrew our 120-square-foot private office in the co-working space. So we moved into a 1,200-square-foot office with a conference room, a private office for the office manager, two bathrooms, and a storage area. And the best part? Now I could take Cooper to work every day!

At this point, I had seven months of business revenue on the books and was able to refinance my personal business loan into a Small Business Association (SBA) loan, which eliminated my obligation to pay commission to my initial investors and it also cut my interest rate in half. I was nervous to tell Eugene and Lucinda that I was ending the loan term early, but they were very understanding (and I think a little proud of me for my progress). The bank paid them, and they were happy to use that money for another investment.

I was now living in a newly remodeled studio apartment above a garage — it was clean and it was mine. It came with a TV hung on the wall, charming old hardwood floors, lots of daylight, and a good-sized porch. I bought a daybed from World Market and my first real mattress for $300 and used this one piece of furniture as a sofa *and* a bed. It was an innovative 2-for-1 deal. I was still recovering from the added overhead costs during my first six months in business, the payment plan I had for my student loans had just increased to $1,200 a month, and I needed a bigger car for work. I was regularly sticking 9 x 12 rugs and large window treatments across my car and out the passenger-side window of my Honda Civic. The plastic covering would flap in the wind so hard that my ears would be ringing until I went to sleep that night. The embarrassment and the noise were one thing, but there were only so many times I could get aggressively beeped at for my dangerous protrusions sticking out from my vehicle. I caved to necessity and bought an SUV. I upgraded to a used Toyota Highlander and was able to keep my car payments the same. I recognized that, to grow my company, I needed to be truly profitable so I could use the extra money and reinvest it back into the business. I was prepared to continue sacrificing in terms of the way I lived for as long as I needed to. In all my decisions — personal and professional — I would keep the business as my first priority. I mean, I was just happy to have a nice place to live. It felt great!

I was romantically single, still actively networking my business, and free-lance writing for *Wrightsville Beach Magazine* once a month. I was seeing my little buddy from the Big Buddy Program almost every weekend after being paired together for five years, and I started an annual fundraiser for a local nonprofit called The Carousel Center. The Carousel Center helps children in our community who have been domestically and sexually abused by providing medical exams, forensic interviews, and trauma therapy. I had planted my roots here in Wilmington, with many strong friendships, a reliable business network, and a sense of community. I was the most fulfilled I had been in a long time.

 I had planted my roots here in Wilmington, with many strong friendships, a reliable business network, and a sense of community. I was the most fulfilled I had been in a long time.

Falling in Love

It had been nine years since I left the house on Birchcroft Road. I still was not speaking to my sister and, luckily, I had not heard from anyone else in the blood-relative category. My relationships now were all healthy ones, and I could finally see a clear correlation between the quality of our relationships and the quality of our lives. I had learned that — in my life, at least — unhealthy relationships were fueled by a lack of self-esteem or the need to heal a past wound, which then propelled widespread toxicity (which showed every warning sign and was felt through intuition, but often ignored until it blew up like dynamite and left me with third-degree burns). Well, that's the *Cliff's Notes* version!

Because I had met my previous boyfriend, Anthony, in the K&M networking group, I often scouted the younger guys in the group as they entered the room. There was one guy (who was not, unfortunately, single) but was the most handsome man

K&M Speed Networking Christmas party with my best friends to this day, Ashley, Lucinda, and Alex

I had ever seen. He had started his business at the same time I had joined the group, back when I was at Exemplify Design. He was a personal trainer, and the name of his gym was RipXFit Fitness Studio. He had a thick South American accent and, while I couldn't understand one word he was saying, there was something about his olive skin, hazel eyes, and warm smile that literally made me too nervous to talk to him and afraid to sit anywhere near him. I could feel his energy and his heart when he spoke. His charisma and presence filled the room, he was genuine, and I saw his passion for what he did. His passion reminded me of mine and his name was Jean-Pierre.

At the meetings, I would talk to every person except for him. Our meetings had anywhere from 30 to 60 people and here I was avoiding one person in the room. This went on until one day my shoulder brushed his while I was trying to traverse the crowd at Strickland's — a blinds, shades, shutters, and draperies company that hosted our meetings once a month. I was so nervous after my shoulder touched his that I ran across the room in embarrassment. I was not a shy or nervous person. This was not like me — at all.

A few weeks later, we had a smaller lunch gathering at a café called Sweet N Savory. Instead of 60 of us, there were only 12 of us at this more intimate networking opportunity. There were three tables of four people each, so when I saw Jean-Pierre at one table, I purposefully chose another. I was sitting next to Laura and we were talking about possibly signing up for a mud run. Jean-Pierre overheard the conversation and came over to talk to us. I could not help but think that he was the most beautiful person I had ever seen. Jean-Pierre told us to come try a class at his gym, which helped people prepare for obstacle races, such as the mud runs. I told him that I was too busy with work to attend the classes, but I was hoping to make exercise a priority again very soon. This was the first time we actually spoke — May 2015.

When I first joined K&M, I had told my friends that I could tell this guy was the best at what he did and that, one day, I would train with him. I just needed it to be the right time. Finally, I was ready. Jean-Pierre and I had been friends on Facebook for over a year (yes, I was still "out there" on Facebook, much to my own surprise!), so I knew he wasn't single. That made me feel more comfortable about attending his classes for the first time. He posted a promotion for a combination of group classes and four personal-training sessions for beginners. I messaged him about joining and told him I would be there the following week.

Attending my first fitness class was a rude awakening regarding how weak I had become. I had worked through the past year without any sort of strength training. I could barely lift 10-pound dumbbells, and doing a pushup seemed like it might break my body. At the class, I made a new friend, Liam, who was also new to class; the two of us were determined to become stronger so we wouldn't be doomed to suffer through these work outs in the future. I didn't like dreading the suffering and I didn't like feeling weak. This gave me immediate goals. I couldn't wait to come back each day because I was seeing quick progress and I clearly observed a correlation between my physical strength, my emotional strength, and my confidence. I loved having goals, but there was also something about Jean-Pierre that made me want to keep coming back. I was connecting with his energy and

his passion; it was like I had met my
match in these two areas ... for the first
time in my life.

*Gym class at RipXFit with my
BFFs, Kellie and Meleah*

In my first personal training session,
I asked Jean-Pierre if I could call him JP
because let's be honest, his name was
too formal and fancy. Honestly, I hated
the name, but that was my short-term
secret. JP was very bossy and I wasn't the
submissive type, but I was too nervous
to be sassy just yet so I did everything
he said — including repeating squats
and knee push-ups over and over and
over until I had perfect form. He was
a perfectionist too, just like me.

During my next physical training session, I asked JP about his girlfriend and
he mentioned they had broken up. He seemed upset about it, so I didn't ask
any further questions. Then I convinced myself to stop dreaming because
I could never date a personal trainer — that just seemed way too cliché. Can
you imagine dating a guy who trains pretty girls all day and his job is just to
make them look *better*? No, thank you!

The Saturday classes at RipXFit were the ones that made people throw
up, but you also didn't want to miss them. Liam, Josh, and I stayed a few
minutes after class to finish our conversation with JP. The four of us made
plans to go to lunch at a place called Bluewater, which overlooked yachts
along the intracoastal waterway, and we made additional plans to go swimming at the beach afterward. I was so nervous to eat in front of my new, hot
trainer, so I ordered a salad. I just couldn't eat what I really wanted to, which
was chicken tenders, French fries, and extra ketchup.

We made it to the beach as the clouds drifted across the sky and it started
sprinkling. Liam and Josh didn't want to go in the water because the sun
wasn't out, but swimming in the ocean gave me this overwhelming sense of
freedom, and I loved these big waves. JP said he was definitely going in, so
he ran in first, which allowed me enough time to take off my dress without
him seeing me in my bathing suit ... and I ran into the water behind him.

I was waist deep when he looked back. I was lifting each leg to push through the heavy water and our eyes locked. Seconds passed, but it seemed like time had stopped and that the raindrops were no longer touching us. My breath halted on inhale — I felt something. *No, this can't be real.* I knew when the mutual glance felt like serendipity that I was going to marry him. My next thought was that I had absolutely gone insane.

JP and I swam for an hour, while the rain was coming down and the waves were gaining height, crashing aggressively on our backs. We were having a blast, but now I was starving, especially after that workout and the iceberg lettuce lunch. I admitted my hunger to Liam, and he admitted his stomach was growling because he, too, hadn't wanted to eat too much in front of our new trainer. Once

The first day JP and I hung out, after our ocean swim, and during JP's first time at Five Guys

everyone admitted they were starving, we decided on Five Guys — a choice that was the opposite of what we all ate in front of our trainer at lunch. But when you reach that certain level of hunger, you start making less rational decisions. JP didn't know what Five Guys was, so we introduced the foreigner to something he would remember forever. After eating hotdogs, hamburgers, and Five Guys fries, we started talking about our plans that night, and I casually invited him to my friend Meleah's house, to which he agreed.

Before I knew it, JP and I had become inseparable. Our first casual date was a trip to the movies the very next day, then our second date was a few nights later. We went to dinner at a downtown pub called Copper Penny, then ran down all the scary alleyways. We shared our first kiss under a pergola that stretched across two buildings in an alley that connects Front and Second Street. He lifted me to hang from the beam and as I came down, his strength made me feel safe and sparks were flying. We continued to kiss across the historic district, inside alleyways, under doorways, and in the gardens of wedding venues, then we tried to say goodbye in the parking garage but we continued to kiss until the early morning hours. Our chemistry was overwhelming. I wasn't sure if I was actually *feeling* or if I had gone numb.

After our first few dates, it was obvious to others in class that we had crushes on each other. He tried to appear professional, because I was a client after all, but he ended up just following me around the gym, showing up at my circuit station each round. I wanted my form to be perfect and I wanted to appear stronger because I knew he was looking at me.

JP invited me over every night after class and we would get subs and salads from the grocery store behind his apartment. We would talk for hours and hours. Our energy together was magnetic. He was the first person I had met who was on my level of loving life and loving people this much. He was a connector too — he had a passion for connecting with people. He was nowhere near "average" — the state of being that I was bound and determined to rise above.

I would try to say no to him about coming over, but I never could, so we would spend hours talking, then I would sleep from midnight to 3:00 a.m., wake up, and finish the work that I was supposed to do the night before. After two weeks of hanging out, JP told me that he knew when he looked at me in the ocean that I was *the one*. I could not believe it. I told him that I felt the same way and I had told my best friend and we both agreed I had gone crazy. *What was happening to me?*

Walls Up

There were so many things about JP that drove me crazy. His ascending laugh was obnoxious, and he had certain mannerisms that I viewed as cocky, narcissistic, and unattractive. He grunted a lot during the Saturday workouts, he liked video games, and he went out to eat three times a day (every day) instead of learning to go grocery shopping. At his apartment, his laundry stayed in the dryer or in the hamper — it was never folded or put away. He would open a cabinet door and refrain from shutting it. My OCD would kick in and I would continually stare at the open doors and, after so many ignored glances (which I thought were subtle hints to him — "hey, you left that door open"), I would need to close them all myself. He drove a Camaro and he drove it way too fast, which also annoyed me. He exhibited selfish bachelor tendencies and my tolerance was pretty low for any ounce of selfishness. Aside from the annoyances, he was different from anyone I had ever met before, and I was intrigued.

I knew JP was different because when he would look at me, I felt like he was seeing my soul ... as if he saw right through me. I mean, he saw through *everything*, and I knew it unequivocally when he said, "You are a robot."

I stared — as I stopped myself from saying FUCK YOU. At first, I didn't say anything at all. As I looked at him and he looked back at me, suddenly I knew that *he* knew. By calling me a robot, he pointed out what no one else had ever actually dared to say: that I was emotionally closed off. I had walls up that were longer and stronger than the Great Wall of China. *But how did he know?*

I felt exposed, and angry. I felt forced to remember where I had been and what I had survived.

When I was in high school, Val (one of my best friends since kindergarten) started to make a new best friend, who was essentially replacing me in her life. This happened the summer after I lived with her, so I figured she probably got sick of me after sharing a twin bed with me for an entire summer. I didn't blame her. Then, she started to date a guy who I had dated for three years. I politely asked her not to date him, not only because of things he had done to me but because I didn't want him to do it to her. I was scared for her.

His name was Jake. After being his best friend for most of our school years, and being more than friends for three years, I finally had had enough when he made his friend pick me up after work and they snuck me into his basement. I thought they wanted to hang out, so I felt OK about sneaking in and doing something innocent, like watching a movie. His friend sat on the couch in front of the television, while Jake asked me to follow him into the other room, which was more of a utility room with the furnace. He then proceeded to make it clear that he had sexual demands and that he wasn't letting me go home until I performed them.

I take a certain amount of responsibility for letting this go too far, but I know it wasn't my fault. I had let him treat me poorly many times before but in this moment, my tolerance for his chronically abhorrent behaviors was worn by the utmost form of disgust. I felt dirty, used, worthless, stupid, and angry. I refused to be treated like this, especially by someone I was choosing to have in my life. I looked at him, told him he was a horrible person (a decision that was better than slapping him), and I walked into the other room of his basement where his friend was. I was shaking from both anger and embarrassment. It was past 11:00 p.m. and I lived two miles away. I told Jake's friend what he said and begged him to take me home, which he did.

In looking back on my teen years and on this high school relationship, in particular, I now realize I was easily manipulated by him because of my lack of self-esteem. I had feelings for him because I knew he had feelings for me, but I always kept him at an arm's reach so I could maintain my control. If I thought he was a good person, I would have had unsolicited feelings for him, but he was consistent in my life and that led me down this path. Obviously, at one point, I had lost momentary control (and safety) and that was when I knew I could never talk to him again.

That was my plan, until Val told me that she was seeing him and asked me if she could officially "date" him. I don't remember if I had told her everything because of my embarrassment, but I had felt I had told her enough for her to make the right decision. When she decided to date him anyway, I remained a supportive friend but their relationship meant I had to see him and, from time to time, hang out with him. Val and I drifted further apart, but then I started to date one of our best guy friends, "Brow," our senior year. He was my first serious boyfriend and we ended up falling in love and staying together for two years, including our freshman year of college. Near graduation, Val told me she needed to talk to me. She asked me to come over and I remember it was right before a Friday-night football game. She was dressed up in school spirit gear and seemed like she was in a rush because her friend, my replacement, was on her way over.

As it turned out, Val wasn't a fan of me dating Brow. She said, "The three of us were best friends and now you are dating him. I think you should stay friends with him, so it doesn't ruin our friendship."

"I would never let it ruin our friendships. If it doesn't work out, I promise I won't let anything happen. I know it is a change, but both of us have boyfriends now and that's bound to change the dynamic of things."

"Danielle, I heard you lost your virginity to him. Is that true?"

"Yes."

"Why didn't you tell me?"

"Because I wanted to tell you in person. It's not like I can just talk about that over the phone."

"Well, it's not like that's the only thing you haven't told me," she retorted. "You never told me anything about your family. All you say is you hate your mom, and then you weren't crying when your dad died, *and* you don't want anything to do with your brother so I let you stay here for a whole summer and I still don't know why. You haven't told me anything and I feel like I am left in the dark on the truth about you."

"I am sorry I just don't talk about that stuff. What do you want to know? I will tell you anything."

"It is too late, Danielle."

Val and I never spoke again. I tried reaching out, but never got a response. I was heartbroken, and I realized that I owed my friends the truth … but the truth was that *no one* knew about my real life, not even my boyfriend of two years.

Fast-forward more than a decade and this pattern of leaving people in the dark was reaching a boiling point. When JP called me a robot, this conversation — from 14 years ago with Val — flashed before me. I started seeing the connection between the relationships I had, the times where I was hurt, and the people who had come into my life. Somehow, JP knew I had secrets and suddenly I was scared for my life; I had a strong feeling he was here to pull those secrets out of me. I saw everything aligning. I kept getting these feelings that JP was going to be the one to heal me from my past. I was terrified. I didn't know how to be healed, or even if it was possible.

I saw everything aligning. I kept getting these feelings that JP was going to be the one to heal me from my past. I was terrified. I didn't know how to be healed, or even if it was possible.

Our magnetism ran deep and I craved being around him because his charisma and humor were infectious. But I also knew he was going to unravel me from my core, so I pursued every way to challenge him and found every excuse to push him away. Subconsciously, I was hell-bent on taking the person who I knew (early on) was the one I was supposed to be with — who I felt was my soulmate, and who I knew would love me in a way I had never been loved — and push him away so he couldn't hurt me and so that I didn't need to feel, at all. It was time to run.

I played it so cool — no, I didn't want to come over; no, I would never actually date a personal trainer (because that's cliché); I would never date someone who spoke Spanish because it was way too hard to learn; no I don't want titles (boyfriend/girlfriend); no I didn't want someone who was previously married; NO, NO, NO, NO! I kept my standards in a place where there was no way JP would qualify, but I could not keep myself away from him. I was so anti-emotion that I was convinced he would eventually let me go, but JP was a competitive athlete and he loved a challenge. I told JP if he could last six months putting up with me, that I would consider being his girlfriend. I was making myself very difficult to love.

Learning to Love

There were two things that really impressed me about Jean-Pierre (who I still insisted upon calling "JP"). JP came to the United States from Santiago, Chile, when he was 26 and had begun living the American dream as an entrepreneur. He came here without knowing English (and having failed English classes in school) but he was undaunted. He showed up to this country ready to shake up his life. When I asked JP why he had decided to move to the United States, his story about seeking "a better life" in America sounded very different from what I've heard from other immigrants. JP said that he grew up very spoiled in Chile and that he wanted a challenge that would humble him. He evaluated his worst-case scenario and felt that if it didn't work out, he could always go back, which he could have after his marriage ended (though he chose to stay). The second thing that impressed me about him was that even after his wife broke his heart in many ways, he was so loyal to her and to their marriage; he was still hopeful they would be able to work it out. I did not personally agree with his strategy because I'm the kind of girl who cuts and runs once someone has hurt or betrayed me, but his loyalty to his marriage and his refusal to give up was something I could surely appreciate.

Over the next few months, I tested the hell out of JP, trying to see if he could handle me or if he would abandon me just like I *knew* he would (because that is what people who love you do, right?). After six months of dating, it was clear to me that JP was more than persistent and he was not going anywhere. He would get me flowers almost every week and write me poems. He would help with Cooper and make sure I always had dinner when I worked late. He met my best friend, Liesl, and brought her a wrapped gift with the DVD of the musical *The Sound of Music* along with a hand-written note. He surprised me on a business trip, when he drove several hours out of the way just to have dinner with me, when he was driving back from a Spartan race in Ohio with a broken ankle. He woke me up on Christmas morning with dozens of gifts that he personally wrapped with color-coordinating bows. It was obvious that he loved me, so I apprehensively relinquished my trust and started showing him that I loved him and that he had passed the test. Showing love was not the problem for me; it was receiving it.

 Showing love was not the problem for me; it was receiving it.

Our relationship continued to grow, and suddenly our living situations changed. JP and I were offered the opportunity to move into our friend Robert's house. Robert was moving to Florida and was looking to rent the house to people he could trust to take good care of it. For us, it was a great opportunity because with our businesses being just a few years old, there was no way we could afford to buy a house but, of course, we wanted one. Robert had a small ranch with three bedrooms, a spacious backyard for Cooper, and the perfect deck for grilling. Robert had filled the freezer with my favorite ice cream — black raspberry chocolate chip Talenti Gelato — and he had filled the fridge with an assortment of beers for JP. We rolled around on the floor, shedding happy tears, because we were so excited, and we were so in love.

We didn't have money to buy a bed, so we set up a queen-sized air mattress in the master bedroom. It was one of those tall ones and, when the bed was made, you couldn't tell that it was an air mattress (but, of course, it didn't have a headboard). We put our $10 yard-sale desks in the front bedroom, which then became our home office. The last bedroom was left for JP. It was going to be his mancave. I set up my World Market daybed in there, aligning the back with pillows, making it look like a sofa, and he was going to put his video games and TV in there.

JP and I enjoyed every second of the "honeymoon stage," as most couples do, which usually fades out after the first year. But ours came to a screeching halt after just one month of living together.

Another Chance at a Family Easter Holiday

In March 2016, my sister called me. She was 20 now and we had not spoken since she last left my apartment two years prior. I knew that if she was calling me, it was probably important, so I picked up. She told me that she was getting kicked out of her apartment because her roommate was doing cocaine and that she couldn't go back home because our brother was living there (and he was using and dealing crack).

"I want to get away from this, Danielle. I need to come live with you."

"OK. I don't want you going back home, so let me talk to my boyfriend because we just moved in together."

"OK."

"But listen. If I let you come here, there is no fucking around, do you understand? There is no lying, no fighting, and you have to get a job. We won't charge you rent for the first three months, and we will let you stay here for as long as you need to until you get on your feet, within reason, and not forever. I mean, we just moved in together and I am about to ask him if he can give up his mancave."

"It is really unsafe here so please let me know ASAP. I need to tell my job and my boyfriend because obviously this is a big deal that I would be leaving the state."

"I will talk to him now and call you tomorrow."

"OK."

"And one more thing ..."

"Yeah?"

"You can't leave this time. Like you did last time. If you leave, it has to be a decision we discuss, not just you disappearing. That really broke my heart."

"I promise I won't do that again. That time I just didn't have any money and you were always working, and I didn't even have my own bed."

"Well, I already have a trip planned for two weeks from now. I will be gone for a week — first I am going to Texas for a baby shower and then to California to see some friends. JP doesn't even know you, so you need to behave, and you need to use that time to find a job so that you have money. I can't feed you forever so please promise me that I can still go on my trip and enjoy it."

"I will, Danielle."

As soon as I asked JP if my sister could move in, he relinquished his brand-new mancave and bought her a plane ticket down to North Carolina. I felt his love now more than ever. We spent the next two days getting my sister's bedroom ready so that when she arrived, she felt welcomed and loved.

My sister arrived and, although I was nervous, I was also very excited. I was willing to move on from our past and move forward. I was excited for her and JP to meet, and I was excited to have a family and this could be the year we get to celebrate Easter together. She was older now, so I assumed she was more mature and would hopefully be grateful for us taking her in.

When she arrived, I took my sister grocery shopping and took her to Walmart to get anything she wanted or needed. It made me happy to spoil her, but I had already started building resentment when she did not say "thank you" as we were checking out. We stopped at RipXFit so she could meet JP, and there was not one word or sign of gratitude to him for buying her flight. Ungratefulness is definitely a trigger for me, so we weren't off to the best start.

During the next few days, JP and I left for work early in the morning and there was no sign of my sister waking up anytime soon. I had texted her to vacuum the house, but when I returned home that night, the house had not been vacuumed. After a few days of JP coming home for his lunch break in the early afternoon, we knew that she was now just waking up. There was no update on her looking for a job and JP told me he thought she might be taking pictures of him. He was suspicious the first time when he was in shorts without a shirt, but then when he walked out of the bathroom in a towel wrapped around his waist, he could have sworn she was sneaking out her phone's camera app to take his picture.

The next Friday made two weeks since my sister arrived. She was interviewing for a nannying position for a wealthy family who had a newborn baby. My sister didn't have a college education (nor did our brother), but she had been working in a daycare center for several years and carried a few certificates. When I got back home, I knocked on her door to find out about the interview.

"Hey, how did it go?"

"Well, it didn't go great because the husband is a complete creep."

"What do you mean he's a creep? Isn't he a well-known doctor?"

"Yes, I think he's a surgeon, but I guess they found some photos of me online and he had them pulled up on his computer when I got there. So basically, he was looking at these photos of me."

"What do you mean he found photos of you online ..."

"Ones that my boyfriend took."

I Googled my sister's name. Everything. Went. Black.

JP woke up. He came into my sister's room and this was the first time he had seen me angry to the degree that my family members make me angry. I could not believe what I was seeing on the internet, but I also could not believe that my sister was this "professional" at playing the victim to where she was blaming the parents of a newborn (who were clearly doing a background check for the safety of their new child) for being creepy when she was taking no responsibility for her actions. She was incapable of seeing the black-and-white issue with this entire scenario!

Because she was living with us, this family also did a background on JP and me, which included our businesses. Now, she was here for two weeks and already doing her level-best to ruin our reputations by tying our public brands with her trashy behavior. I told my sister that she had to delete these completely inappropriate pictures off the internet, and she refused.

The yelling turned into screaming (the way we were taught to communicate with each other) and by the time JP was trying to calm us down, my sister started threatening suicide. She flung herself against the bed, in a dangerous three-hour tantrum, screaming and crying while threatening to end her life, right then and there.

The next morning, I called her therapist in Massachusetts. I asked for help and assistance after explaining her suicidal threats from the night before. He refused to help me over the phone because it was violating patient privacy, but he encouraged me to call the police based on her recent threat. I calmly went into her bedroom and asked her if she was on any medication. At that point, she told me that she ran out of the medication she was on when she came down here. I did *not* sign up for this!

I hated to leave JP with my sister at this point, but I had this trip planned and I was not going to let her take this away from me. JP promised me that it was going to be fine and that he was taking her out for sushi so they could talk things out. We told my sister that our one rule was she could not have anyone we didn't know come over to our house (which at this point was everyone), and that she was never allowed to have anyone over while we weren't home.

After one night of being in Texas, I received a call from JP telling me that my sister had snuck out and then came home at 2 o'clock in the morning, audibly drunk and accompanied by a random guy. Meanwhile, she was still "with" her boyfriend in Massachusetts. I thought JP would have handled the situation the way I would have — get up, kick what's-his-name out of our house and talk to my sister in the morning. But he didn't and now I was mad at both of them. "*So you left for work with a random guy sleeping in our house???*" I tried to have some sympathy because this wasn't his sister and he was not prepared to handle these situations, so I told him he needed to talk to her on his lunch break about her lack of respect toward us and that if this happened again, we would call the cops. JP had a firm conversation with my sister and made it clear that she was to get a job, clean the house when we asked, and respect us and our rules. My sister left the gym and called me to see if JP had said anything about last night. I told her I knew what had happened, but I wanted to discuss it when I got back to North Carolina. Then she told me that he made it all up because, as she explained melodramatically, he was cheating on me and this was his way of turning the blame onto someone else. Then she drove to my office, unannounced. She cried to my employees and said that JP threatened to beat her. I couldn't even wrap my head around this insanity.

The next day my friend Meleah went to pick up my sister to take her to the movies; she knew I was out of town and was trying to help keep my sister entertained while I was absent. When Meleah pulled in the driveway, my sister was unashamedly walking out of my house with a different guy, while JP was not home.

Many of these colorful details weren't shared with me while I was away because no one wanted to ruin my vacation, but after one quiet day, I found out, and I started putting everything together. The pictures of JP without a shirt on, putting our reputations in jeopardy, driving under the influence to our house, sneaking in guys, cheating on her boyfriend, lying about my boyfriend, invading my company, and trying to ruin everything I had going for me for the first time in my life. I was DONE — with the lies, the ungratefulness, and her using me over and over and over again. I loved her and I wanted to help her, but she made it impossible.

I tried booking a flight home, but there was nothing under $1,000, which was money I did not have. I called my sister. I told her I knew everything, and I told her that she was to stay at the house until JP got home. JP came home on his lunch break and there was no sign of my sister. She had disappeared once again.

We saw that she stole all our camping gear out of the garage. Her boyfriend from Massachusetts contacted me and said that she was driving back to Massachusetts and he knew something was wrong when she said that we had kicked her out. We shared our truths, and it was the most complex spider web of lies I had ever witnessed in the spinning and that I had ever had the displeasure of trying to explain to someone else. She was manipulating all of us for her own benefit. My sister had been at our house for three weeks and it had turned into a complete nightmare.

As for my budding romance with JP, this experience changed the tone of our relationship. JP felt like he had been through a tornado and I was triggered in the form of a time capsule, where I was brought right back to being inside the dark doors and closed windows at 99 Birchcroft. Our relationship waxed and waned as our triggers and insecurities started to peek through; I was completely exposed for the first time. My pot had boiled over.

Facing My Past

I couldn't look at the chair.

It was our first session. Marcia asked me to look at the chair and pretend it was "my mother." I kept trying to just look at the chair, but I couldn't. I cowered, bringing my knees into my chest while breathing deeper and deeper into a wretched state of panic. I was crying, breathing heavier and louder, trying to stop because I was so embarrassed that I could not complete this simple task.

She took the chair away and said, "I know where we need to start now. We have a lot of work to do."

When I was 29, I was referred to a woman named Marcia who was a holistic and energetic psychologist. She uses an energy psychology called advanced integrated therapy (AIT), a practice commonly used with patients who have suffered a trauma and/or are experiencing post-traumatic stress disorder (PTSD). As I understood it, AIT hinged on the theory that the subconscious buries emotional trauma and can often cause *physical* impairments and illnesses. To release the emotional trauma, we must first unearth it from our subconscious and then work to release the stored trauma from our physical body.

At first, she would calibrate my energy. She used a pendulum and had me do a few grounding positions where I would twist my legs and arms together while sitting and then press my tongue backward onto the roof of my mouth.

Then, she would use my arm as a way to tune into the subconscious. My muscles were smarter than my brain because they were connected to the subconscious, something I didn't think was possible, until I sat in this room and experienced it. If my arm fell, it meant that statement was false. If my arm remained stiff in the air, what I was saying was true and it aligned with my subconscious. It was my subconscious making the decisions, not me. While I was thinking and responding with an answer, my arm would show the opposite. I wasn't being true to myself or acting and speaking in my own best interests.

 It was my subconscious making the decisions, not me. I wasn't being true to myself or acting and speaking in my own best interests.

I would stick out my arm, very stiff and strong, clenching a fist. She would make easier statements to start. I would repeat them after her.

"My name is Snow White."

She would lightly tap my arm and it would fall fast.

"My name is Danielle."

My arm remained stiff in the air.

"I have love toward men."

My arm would fall.

"I don't want men to suffer for the pain they have caused me."

My arm would fall.

"I love myself."

My arm would fall.

When my arm fell, we had work to do. I would have to repeat the statement with my eyes closed and my hands resting over each chakra (energy center of my body), starting with my crown (head) and moving down the body. I would have to sit on my hands for the final grounding chakra. If I felt choked up, released tears, or felt anger in a certain chakra, I would have to repeat the statement 10 times. Many times, I could identify where the trauma was stored in my body — sometimes it was my heart or solar plexus and other times it was my maternal side of the body, the right side, or the paternal side of the body, the left side. There wasn't a part of my body that was free and clear.

Before I started repeating the statement, I would rate how much emotion I felt, on a scale of 1 to 10. At the end, I had to be at a 2 or less to move on. Sometimes we would spend a whole session on one trigger phrase, and it took 18 months to work through two dozen.

During one session, as I was counting to 10, holding my hand over my heart chakra, I had a vision. It was a memory — one I had not recalled in 20 years. The Lady was angry and she took our socks off our feet and pushed us out the front door, locking us outside during a snowstorm. The stairs and pathway were covered in several inches of ice. It was dark outside, and I remember my brother and me freezing, standing on the ice. I remember the sensation of the coldness in my soul — the emotional pain of this cruelty and abuse — as rendering me frozen that went far beyond the weather conditions.

In my mind, sitting there in Marcia's office during my therapy session, I could see us standing there, in shock. I can still see us now. We were in our pajamas. "Fight or flight" kicked in and we pulled our pants over our feet and sat down on the ice because it was less painful than standing.

Depending on how much I was disassociating — a coping mechanism in which I was leaving my body to avoid feeling the emotional aspect of my body — Marcia would have me do a few positions until my head was fluttering and I felt more grounded. Sometimes I would check out and dissociate and she could see it happening before I realized it. She would say, "You're floating again, come back Danielle, come back."

I was starting to remember these things. The traumatic experiences were popping out of my subconscious and showing me visuals — I could see myself experiencing the abuse. What did this mean?

I remember hearing the letters "PTSD" again, disconnecting and detaching myself from a label or diagnosis. Marcia explained that I was dissociating myself or leaving my body during these traumatic experiences as part of a survival mechanism. Living in denial was comfortable. That's where I was. Everything was fine. I was FINE. I WAS OVER IT! I had survived — what more did I need to do?

 The traumatic experiences were popping out of my subconscious and showing me visuals — I could see myself experiencing the abuse. What did this mean?

Triggered

The past stays in the past, until it doesn't.

One day, two years into my relationship with JP, I was driving my car when I saw a couple — a young man and woman — in the middle of the street. It was around 3:00 p.m. on a Saturday afternoon. I saw his arm lash out violently toward her body.

No ....

I slowed down. He pushed her and then his arm punched her again.

I looked around. *Why is no one else seeing this except for me???*

My heart was racing. I turned my car around and drove closer toward them. I could see they were younger than me.

I approached them and saw his body language immediately change. I rolled down my window.

Firmly but calmly, I asked, "Hi, what is going on?"

He ran. He sprinted down the street and into the woods.

"I don't know what's wrong with him. He's acting so jealous and accusing me of being a slut. We have a baby together," she said, sounding like she was apologizing or mourning (or both).

I thought about all the possible victims and asked, "Where's the baby?"

"At home with my mom. We just moved into my parents' house." Her eyes were darting around the street and the nearby woods, as if she was expecting him to come back and she needed to be ready.

"He hit you," I said, like a protective big sister. "Why is he hitting you? You can't let him hit you. You don't deserve this."

"I know," she said, then launched into excuses for him. "He has been a lot better, really. I don't know what's wrong with him today. He started acting crazy again. He is on probation ... PLEASE don't call the cops, we have a baby and ..."

"I saw him hit you," I said again. "I can't let this happen to you. I am sorry, but I need to call the cops."

Our conversation had lasted probably less than a minute, but it felt like a lifetime. My need to intervene and rescue her from her abusive situation was as much about me as it was about her. I had spent my *own* lifetime not being rescued. How could people possibly look the other way and "mind their own business" when people were being hurt? I would not do — to this girl — what an entire community had done to me.

At this point, another car pulled over, driven by a young man who identified himself as working for the government and having also witnessed the young woman being assaulted. He called the police.

Once the police arrived, I said goodbye to the girl. She looked at me as if she was as upset with me as she was with the boyfriend who had struck her. In that moment, I felt struck too.

I went home and told JP what had happened. I got through the retelling of the story just fine until I went to go put laundry in the washer and felt my feet go numb and my breath got heavier. I started to hyperventilate, dropping the laundry, and crawling to the living room carpet where I started kicking, screaming, and crying as if it was me that had been hit. I was triggered.

I had not had an anxiety attack since high school. JP watched me on the floor, looking like I was having an emotional seizure. The feeling sat with me for days. I was grieving for this girl I did not know. I was thinking about their baby, while my subconscious was about to explode.

I was not only grieving for her; I was grieving for myself. It was all starting to make sense.

 I was not only grieving for her; I was grieving for myself. It was all starting to make sense.

Traffic

The traffic lights field chaos,
separating the severity of each case.
My comfort lies in the green,
as I race through the days,
fitting in as much as I can,
and suppressing the warning signs
that there is an accident ahead.

13

Red Light

I started therapy at the age of 29. I certainly could have used it sooner but, like most of us do, I waited until I hit rock bottom. I spent 18 months with Marcia — doing heavy, deep, and dark work. It got worse before it got better. I was emotionally drained and physically exhausted. Our weekly visits were like being thrown in a cage of lions, where the only way out was to look the lions straight in the face and say, *"You can let me go now. I am not afraid of you anymore."*

Ideally, I would be going through something like this while I was single, but that was not the case. JP had been watching me unravel, and the problem was that when I was triggered, it would trigger his triggers. We were a volatile, emotional pair.

JP grew up in the upper middle class for most of his childhood. He had a nanny who cared for him and his two sisters and they had a maid who cleaned the house. His mother stayed at home but would rely on the nanny to care for her children, primarily because she struggled with mental health issues that weren't addressed medically until she and JP's father divorced, when JP was 18. As he explains it, JP would frequently shut down emotionally when his mother raised her voice or when her unpredictable behavior caught him off-guard. There was no telling what the result might be after she raised her voice, as her ability to regulate her words and actions was unreliable, at best. One minute, she was going on as if he was the most beautiful and perfect son, and then next minute she would be slapping him across the face for incorrectly reciting his ABC's.

JP's father was the provider of the family, which meant he was not home much. He was a good provider — he paid for his children's sports, private school tuition, and their college educations. JP saw his parents fight frequently and when a fight started, he recalls watching his dad pack a bag and leave for the night, later sneaking back in his bed with him the next morning, hiding out with the children rather than facing his wife.

Burned Out

It is no secret that the first few years of starting a company are stressful. I was still working inhumane hours and sacrificing myself and my relationship to take a backseat to making sure my company made it to year three. I was under-rested, eating poorly, and not allowing myself to participate in the things that brought me joy. There were things that I wanted but couldn't afford, like a real bed. I had been sacrificing for so long now, and I was tired of being broke and tired of being tired. Any extra energy I had went toward the rehashing of everything in my past and dealing with it, week after week, but I had no energy left for my relationship.

> I was still working inhumane hours and sacrificing myself and my relationship to take a backseat to making sure my company made it to year three. I was under-rested, eating poorly, and not allowing myself to participate in the things that brought me joy.

JP had expanded his gym into a new building that almost quadrupled his square footage. Because he needed a business loan for the new equipment to fill this new space, he was in debt for the first time in his life. His overhead costs were high, with a beautiful building on a main road in a desirable location. I was conditioned to being in debt and I had a high tolerance for stress, but he did not. I was conditioned to thrive under these conditions, but while I was begging my classmates for lunch money, JP was being fed gourmet meals by his personal chef. This kind of struggle — financial struggle — was new to him.

I had little sympathy for his lack of tolerance. We would get home from work and it would be late, and we were hungry and tired. A stupid fight would start and within minutes, I would raise my voice, then JP would have his bag packed and be out the door and back at the gym. He would sleep on an air mattress there and would not come home. Each time this happened, my resentment built up higher and higher, which caused the frequency to double, then triple. Sometimes, JP would leave for a night and come back the next night like nothing happened. Sometimes it would be several nights before he came back home. Sometimes I would hear from him — getting calls and/or texts while we were apart. Sometimes he would not contact me or answer me for a few days. When the gym got too cold, he would stay with his friend Rola. I would still show up for my class at the gym and we would ignore each other.

Each scenario drove me insane but being left day after day, week after week, triggered me even more. Now, I felt abandoned by the person I loved the most. I was hurt and unheard. I had lost control, and I didn't like feeling out of control of *any* situation, especially an emotional one. I told JP that he, too, needed therapy, but he refused; his refusal fueled our next sequence of fights.

 I felt abandoned by the person I loved the most.

I cooked up a "solution" — or at least my next move in this dysfunctional game of emotional chess. In the moment, it seemed like a great idea. The next time JP came home after disappearing for a few days, I would have all his clothes on the front lawn. I was not going to let him leave me again; I would just kick him out. It shouldn't have been a power war, but it was, because neither of us was being rational. We were emotionally triggered, which then triggered each other, which turned into a vicious cycle of the serial abandoner boyfriend and the serial kicking-you-out girlfriend. Our fights now were about our fights. They did not have real subjects, like money, religion, politics, children, or household chores. It would all happen so fast that I think we'd both admit that we didn't even know what the original cause was. The only subject I actually remember disagreeing about was that JP's client was selling our dream house, and even though we both wanted it, JP agreed with his client when he told us that we could never afford it. I believed the price would lower into our price range, but JP didn't see this as being possible (because we needed the asking price to come down another $200,000). I was a dreamer and stubborn to boot; JP was a realist.

 ## Our fights now were about our fights.

I have heard it said that "hurt people hurt people" and this truth was playing out in my life in significant ways. I had been hurt for decades at a time, and now I was perpetuating that infliction of pain on the man I loved. And the more I hurt JP, the more he reciprocated by being hurtful to me in return. We both had emotional wounds when we met, and now we were subjecting one another to that pain. It was a vicious cycle.

As this toxic dance persisted, I started to kick JP out of the house in more aggressive ways. Once, I left everything he owned outside the door of the gym in the rain. Then I started breaking up with him each time. Even though we fought hard, we loved hard, and no matter what transpired, JP always kept coming back. I let him move back in once he agreed to start seeing Marcia for therapy.

Believe it or not, this went on for about a year. I never had much patience to begin with, but at the end of this exhausting year, we were both spending thousands of dollars we did not have (on therapy) and we were reliving through our painful past memories, which was only adding to our stress levels. I was jaded now. JP and I were seeing Marcia separately *and* together, and Marcia challenged us to agree to a "relationship reset." We had been given the tools to break the trigger cycle and we were supposed to be practicing these commitments and employing the tools at home.

JP had promised he would never leave the house again. He could leave to walk or run or do something physical to help him contend with his fight-or-flight feelings, but he could not pack his bag and leave the house.

I felt a sense of security in this new arrangement. Then one day, I heard the closet door slam open, shadowed by the zipper noise from his duffel bag, followed by the jingle of his keys. These three noises sang a song. It was worse than nails on a chalkboard because, by

1947 Quonset Hut, the third location of Port City Design Group and my temporary home

the time I heard the duffel bag zipper, the anger would poison me so fast that I would lose all conscious control of my emotions. This time would be the last time. Not only did he do it again, but he broke his promise again. I was done. I called my friend and colleague Joe (who knew a thing or two about moving because he was officially my firm's installer/mover) and together we moved all my stuff into the warehouse of my new office. I had a sofa now, so we put that in the upstairs design loft, and I spent the next three winter months living a secret life on a couch, in the upstairs of a 1947 Quonset hut.

I had no intention of my colleagues or friends finding out that I was home-less again. So Joe and I had covered all my personal things in the warehouse so that no one at work would find out. I spent December and January (including Christmas and New Year's) living on a couch with a space heater in front of me so Cooper and I could sleep. I told my employees I was getting a new sofa for the house and that is why I moved this one into the office. Each morning, I would hide my pillow and my comforter in the storage closet. I hung my clothes on a rolling cart, hung my shoe organizer from the pole on the cart, and put a cover over it so that each morning I would wake up, uncover my wardrobe to grab fresh clothes, and then cover the evidence like it never happened. I had a mini fridge, which worked just fine. I had started following a nutritionist's meal plan which made it even more believable to my employees that I was "meal prepping" and needed all the ingredients at work. I did not have a shower, only a sink, so I would go to Joe's house every other day for a shower, and on the in-between days I would wipe myself down with wet face cloths and baby wipes.

It was cold, but it was peaceful and calm. I had detoxed off sugar and I was thinking and seeing clearer. My energy had shifted again because I felt myself shedding weight — physically, emotionally, and spiritually. I was climbing out of the dark clouds, never feeling the anticipated loneliness. I enjoyed the silence and, really, the love and companionship from Cooper could get me through anything.

I felt myself shedding weight — physically, emotionally, and spiritually. I was climbing out of the dark clouds, never feeling the anticipated loneliness. I enjoyed the silence and, really, the love and companionship from Cooper could get me through anything.

Trusting, Rebuilding, Embracing a New Life

Surely, I have some regrets about the tumultuous start to my relationship with JP — things I did and said that I wish I hadn't. But as I look back to how it all played out, I am so grateful I took another round of homelessness for this time to myself. I was healing and closing my old wounds, which were only being reopened and exposing themselves for more grief by attempting to be part of an intimate partnership at the same time. My past chased me down and gave me a red light. I could not love JP if I did not love myself. I could not love myself if I did not heal from my past, which I had suppressed and never dealt with. It followed me everywhere I went, for a long time, until it tackled me to the floor and forced me to deal with it, right then and there.

My past chased me down and gave me a red light. I could not love JP if I did not love myself.

I don't think I met JP at the perfect time in our lives. I don't think we were ready for each other, but we were blessed to find each other, and perfect timing is a luxury we weren't given. I knew he would challenge me, I knew he would love me unconditionally, and I knew he would be part of my healing process — but I did not realize he would need the same from me, at the same time.

In due time, JP and I were back to living under the same roof. But it wasn't in a house. I went from living in my office to living at JP's gym, RipXFit. Our friend Robert — whose house we had been renting — wanted to put the house up for sale because the market was strong, and we opted to move out and live in the gym temporarily to help us save for a down-payment on a house. We slept on our trusted air mattress, but it popped on the second night, so JP slept on a twin air mattress and I slept on the stretching table, which is a lot like sleeping on a yoga mat lying on pavement. We were humbled and we were happy.

*February 17, 2018 — JP proposed to me at the same spot
on the beach where we first felt sparks*

On February 17, 2018, JP proposed to me, very unexpectedly, at the same beach access where our eyes locked and our souls connected while we were swimming in the waves for the first time in June 2015. The day he proposed, I was in sweatpants and had not showered, and it was perfect. He started reading a poem to me, which was the second in a trilogy. The third poem would be unveiled on our wedding day. As he read the proposal poem, he started to cry. At this point, I had no idea he was going to propose; in fact, I assumed he was emotional because he felt guilt or regret for how we had hurt each other. Then I saw our friend Mitch taking pictures from behind the sand bank. JP pulled out a book he made, titled "To My Future Wife," which had poems, stories, and photos of our past three years together. Of course, I said *yes*!

Three weeks later, I was working late and had Cooper with me at the office. I knew something was wrong when he didn't get up and follow me to the bathroom. I had taken him to the vet that morning because he had been vomiting the night before. They did a full exam and injected him with fluids for slight dehydration and gave him anti-nausea medicine. They told me he was perfectly fine, and at first I thought maybe he was drowsy from the medicine, but when I heard his deep and rapid breathing, my heart sank.

I went over to him — he was lying in his bed by my feet under the desk. He was not responding to me. I started to scream his name, but Cooper did not wake up.

I Google-searched "dog in coma" and Google told me to lift up his lips and if the color of his gums was white then he was in severe distress, possibly even in a coma. I lifted his lips and his gums were white.

I screamed like I was being murdered, as I got into my car and kept Cooper's limp body draped over my knees. I barely remember how I got to the emergency vet, but I do remember calling my friend Kellie, because JP kept his phone on silent while he was sleeping. Kellie went to the gym to bang on the glass to wake up JP, and they both met me at the animal hospital.

I ran through the double doors screaming, "SOMEBODY HELP MEEE!! HELP ME!!!!!"

The vet took Cooper and when we were called into the room, she told us he had been in anaphylactic shock. She suspected it was an allergic reaction to a fire-ant bite, but there was no evidence of a flared-up bite, just a small scab on his front paw. Cooper's liver enzymes were reading off the charts and the only possible solution was a plasma transfusion. I looked at the vet and told her that I would chop off my arm to save his life, and that I expected her to do whatever she needed to do to save my dog. She had to save my dog.

Cooper started to seize during the first round of plasma. His brain was bleeding and he was, as I understand it, essentially going brain dead. The vet wheeled him back into the room on a gurney and I held him while he was euthanized. I could not let go of him. I had just lost the first love of my life.

The next day was the only "sick day" I ever remember taking. JP and I were up all night, and while he wanted to work so he didn't have to think about our loss, I was completely non-functional.

Family photo, our last year with Cooper

I stayed at RipXFit with my swollen face and my sweatshirt soaked with tears and I cried, screamed, hyperventilated, and questioned why my 6-year-old dog was just taken from me tragically, way too soon.

That night, we both had this feeling come over us — what if Cooper left me now because he felt his job was done? What if he felt that I had someone to love me and take care of me and that he knew I would be OK now? It was like Cooper was passing me off to JP.

Still Searching for "Home"

We were struggling without Cooper, and not having a place to live didn't make it any easier. After living in the gym for a month, I could not handle the poor sleep, cold nights, or cold showers. Our friend Meleah had just moved out of her friend's furnished rental, so she helped us get in on a month-to-month basis. We were hesitant to sign a long-term lease because we were hopeful we would get our dream house soon.

When I lived in the apartment that flooded, I used to go running in the neighborhood of Forest Hills. It was the most iconic, picturesque neighborhood I had seen. The curved live oaks overhung the streets, dripping in Spanish moss. The houses varied from historic colonials to charming ranches and large Tudors. The neighborhood was built in the '40s and '50s and was known for its Mr. Rogers "beautiful day in the neighborhood" feel. Parents would walk with the kids (hand-in-hand or pulled by wagon) down the street to Forest Hills Elementary in the mornings, and the mailman completed his delivery route by foot, passing the families on their way from school in the afternoons. I would dream about living in this neighborhood one day, and the architectural charm of each house was especially alluring to me as an interior designer.

When I sent an email to our realtor, James, in 2017, it contained a lot of parameters. This is an excerpt of our wish list, in the category of "must-haves:"

- ✓ We both love mid-century modern and minimalist design. We hate clutter and closed spaces with outdated materials.

- ✓ House with lots of windows and natural daylight!!!

- ✓ No new-construction, cookie-cutter houses. I would love an older home with character and, of course, I can make it mid-century modern. Houses built in the 1950s would be great!

- ✓ The yard is everything. We need trees. The bigger and older, the better.

- ✓ Dark hardwood floors or concrete underneath that we can finish and polish.

- ✓ Potential neighborhoods: Forest Hills, anywhere off Masonboro Loop Rd./Greenville Loop Rd. or Middlesound Loop Rd.

Then JP remembered that his client of several years had his former house on the market. He told me it was the best backyard he had ever seen in his life. We found the listing and I could not believe it. The house was in Forest Hills, and only five houses away from the Mr. Rogers-style neighborhood ele-

Dream home

mentary school. The house was built in 1949, it sat on a 1.2-acre lot, it had dark hardwood floors that were original to the house with floor-to-ceiling windows spanning the back and overlooking a pond surrounded by old-growth trees. It was beyond idyllic.

Falling in love with this house involved some initial heartbreak. It was an emotional fight that lasted more than a year, but the price of the home eventually dropped to where JP and I needed it to be, and the law of attraction worked in our favor. From the second I saw the pictures on the realtor's website, I could see us raising our family in this house. I could see our Christmas tree in the front window, and I could see us getting married on the island in the middle of the pond in the big backyard. I never lost faith. We hustled at work to get our down payment and we closed on May 18, 2018. The dream home was ours.

Wedding day, June 1, 2019 –
Creating our own family

One month after we moved into our new home, we opened our hearts to a precious dog named Cruz. We were still devastated about losing Cooper, but Cruz was helping us heal by allowing us to fall in love again. One year later, on June 1, 2019, we shared our favorite day — our wedding day — with more than 200 of our friends who had become family. While most of JP's family was unable to make the trip from Chile, he had one cousin travel from Chile with his family to attend our wedding as a groomsman. The other 240 guests were not blood related. We had created our family here in Wilmington and I have never felt more love than I did on that day.

SLOW THE HELL DOWN – The Message of 2020

I was late. I wasn't late for an appointment. I was late for that time of the month. I had just come off the birth control pills that I'd been taking for more than a decade, so I simply assumed my hormones were imbalanced and causing the initial delay of menstruation. At first, I didn't give it much thought. While having dinner with some close friends, I told them I was late but that I'd been having cramps so I was sure we'd be back to "life as usual" come tomorrow. The next day, I was checking vigilantly for evidence that I was not, in fact, pregnant. Eventually, I called my friend Kellie, who was currently at home with her newborn, Casler. Kellie assured me that it was probably stress causing the delay, but she gave the "just in case advice" of taking a test.

A *pregnancy* test?! I had never taken one. "You mean buy one, in a store, by myself?" I was a married, 32-year-old — precisely the expected market for family planning — and yet I was so embarrassed to go buy a pregnancy test.

I stopped at the pharmacy and, luckily, it was empty and quiet. I couldn't *just* buy a pregnancy test — putting just that one item on the check-out counter seemed so conspicuous — so I bought a bag of those peach candies covered in sugar, which I probably eat once every five years.

I went to Kellie's house to take the test, and she told me the test would take three minutes. Her husband held the baby, and she held my hand in her bathroom while I peed on the stick. I stood up to pull up my pants and I heard her stutter the words, "umm ... Danielle, you *might* want to look ..."

As I looked over to the plastic device resting on the bathroom countertop, me with my underwear and pants still right above my knees, I saw a word I was not ready to see: PREGNANT.

I screamed so loud that Kellie's cats moved to the outside of the door to investigate the clamor. I hugged her while I continued to scream, cry, and hyperventilate. *That was three seconds, NOT three minutes. There was no doubt in this stick. My pee was positive, but I was negative.*

I thought I could plan this moment. I wanted kids, but I wanted them on my own terms.

I AM NOT READY.

How far along am I?

I'm about to get fat.

I AM NOT READY FOR THAT EITHER.

I had only been married for five months! What happened to enjoying the year of newlywed bliss? By my estimate, I was about six weeks along.

For me, discovering I might be pregnant was scary, but not for the normal, expected reasons. I get that it's never the "right" time — that even for women and couples who are planning for a child, it's still scary. But for me, there was perhaps nothing that rattled me more than the sense that I was out of control. There are a few things that are embedded in my DNA: I like to be in control, I like things neat and clean, and I crave routine and structure. I am definitely what the experts call a "Type A" personality. I just consider it being the opposite of the lady who gave birth to me.

 There are a few things that are embedded in my DNA: I like to be in control, I like things neat and clean, and I crave routine and structure.

This scenario — becoming pregnant just as we were settling into our marriage, in a new home, with a new dog, still building our businesses — was completely going against all of these things. I didn't get to plan this. I felt a lack of control over my own body. My daily and weekly routine was about to end (or change immensely) and how the heck could I *prepare* if I was already six weeks into this? There was not enough time!

This was overwhelmingly overwhelming, but what it really boiled down to is that I now felt the most immense pressure I would ever face: the pressure to be the opposite of the lady who gave birth to me. I was convinced that I had to *be the best mom* because I *had the worst mom.* My whole life had led me to this moment. I had to become someone — an amazing mom — who I imagined in my head for most of my life. There was no time to process this; I was already six weeks in, ready or not. I wasn't ready to tell JP, but Kellie told me I had to. She was right, but I knew he was going to be thrilled and I would feel so lonely in my emotional hurricane of triggers, fear, and pressure.

JP was 40 years old and wanted to be a dad yesterday. I was 32 and hoping I could stall him as long as possible. I walked in the door with mascara running down my red cheeks. I showed him the test and he fell to the floor, shouting that this was the best day of his life and that this was everything he had always wanted. While he was crying with joy, I was crying beneath a cloud of fear.

I contacted four people that night:

My insurance agent. *When is my hospitalization policy effective?*

My photographer. *I need to capture my body where it is now. Need you ASAP. Monday?*

My two friends who knew I was waiting for my period to come. *I'm pregnant.* Nothing more, nothing less.

I woke up the next morning and JP was eating breakfast with my pregnancy test. The test was propped up against a flower vase, facing him, with that one word in all capital letters blaring at me as I walked by.

P-R-E-G-N-A-N-T

I ate my loneliness away with carbs. Suddenly, the only thing I could eat was bread and pasta. I could not drink sparkling water anymore and I was nauseated from the time I woke up until the time I went to bed. I was covered in eczema for the first time in my life and I was itching for as many hours as I was battling the nausea. What happened to that rumored amazing pregnancy glow? I WAS NOT GLOWING!

Six weeks pregnant, photo shoot to document my pre-pregnancy body, as a keepsake and reference for my future body-back goals

I comfortably lived in denial until my first ultrasound, which was at 10 weeks. Miscarriages ran in my family and my two best friends had just experienced several, so I figured it was better to eliminate any and all emotions until I hit the 12-week mark. And if there's anything I was an expert at it was shutting off my emotions. So for those four weeks or so after the positive pregnancy test, I carried on as normally as I could, not really processing all the implications of starting a family.

As I quickly learned, the ultrasound tech at the obstetrician's office doesn't mess around. She jumped right into her work, rolling the ultrasound transducer over my belly situation, and I started to cry. This was real. Now I have to face this. The denial stage is over.

"I don't see a baby," she said, softly but clearly.

A full-term sac, a growing belly, and raging hormones, but the blueberry never became the gummy bear. There were no arms or legs. It was not time.

When the Body Says No

My body thought I was still pregnant, so I was told I had to induce a miscarriage, otherwise I could wait up to another two months for my body to expel the pregnancy tissue on its own, which would put me at five months pregnant with no baby. I had already miscarried 7-10 days ago, and my body didn't seem to know it yet. This whole thing was creepy. I wanted it to be over.

The at-home induced miscarriage sounded more peaceful than a dilation and curettage (D&C) surgery. I was to insert pills vaginally and then 10 minutes later I would start to cramp, for a process that would take 24-48 hours. I waited until Saturday morning — December 21, 2019 — so I could finish the work week and stay on lockdown for two days.

I kept going pee because I was nervous about how much bleeding I would experience. About an hour in, I remember flushing the toilet and feeling light-headed. I started to ask JP to look up the side effects of the medication, but then I woke up on the tile floor, covered in toilet water, with a huge bump on my head and completely disoriented. I could barely open my eyes and I began to get sick, uncontrollably, and consecutively. By the time I managed to change my clothes, I got sick again and then wet myself at the same time. Not only did I lose all control, but I became non-functional. My head hurt. I had yet another concussion.

Of course, JP and I were never warned about this possibly happening. We called the hospital hotline to find out if this was a normal reaction to the medication. They told us to come in immediately. JP carried me down the stairs, into the car, and into the emergency room. I was dangling in his arms, with my eyes closed and in more physical pain than I had ever experienced.

It was the Saturday before Christmas, mid-afternoon, and the emergency room was at their maximum capacity. JP put me in a wheelchair and wheeled me to the desk. They asked me for my name, and I got out "Danielle" before JP scooped me up in his arms again and started running, because I got sick again.

For the first two hours, my blood pressure hovered around 80/50, too low to even get an IV inserted. The nurse told me they couldn't do anything for me until my BP rose closer to a normal level. I kept begging for help, for something for the pain — but no narcotics, because I was deathly afraid of those. I was using all my energy to scream, while my eyes were closed and I slipped in and out of consciousness. JP thought he was watching his wife die, right in front of him, right before Christmas, my least favorite holiday.

After spending eight hours in the emergency room and experiencing pain I can only dream isn't as bad as actual labor, I was released due to the passing of the placenta, which was confirmed through the ultrasound.

Emotionally, I was stable. I never allowed myself to connect with the situation. I told myself that if I made it to 12 weeks, I would allow myself to get excited. I had six weeks to live in denial and then I would transition into another set of emotions. The only emotion I had processed was fear. Physically, I was unhealthy. My body was repairing itself and it felt like I was very sick. I wasn't sure if my side effects were normal post-miscarriage because none of the doctors had seen this allergic reaction to the medication used to induce the miscarriage. Just like with the pregnancy, I felt like something was off.

I made an emergency appointment with a holistic doctor who I trusted. I told her to run all the bloodwork possible and I showed her the rashes that were covering my body, head to toe. We discussed the expected — medical history, birth control, antibiotic usage, etc. At the most, I was expecting to be anemic again and that would be an easy fix.

Two hours later, I received a voicemail from Dr. Holler. She was adamant that I take a test for Lyme disease. She said that being from Massachusetts and having many tick bites and now a mysterious miscarriage was a familiar scenario for her. She had treated many women who had multiple and consecutive mysterious miscarriages. In many cases, she explained, the culprit was actually dormant Lyme disease, a silent killer.

Well, Dr. Holler was right. I tested positive for Western Blot Lyme disease, band 41. I also had active EBV (mono) along with liver bacteria that was backed up into my bloodstream and many other side effects from these core illnesses, including vitamin deficiencies, anemia, etc.

I had hit another red light. Life was saying "slow down" — or, better yet, "stop." After a lifetime of go-go-go, run-run-run, work-work-work, survive-survive-survive, my body was saying "no."

I had hit another red light. Life was saying "slow down" — or, better yet, "stop." After a lifetime of go-go-go, run-run-run, work-work-work, survive-survive-survive, my body was saying "no."

I spent the next year adding doctors' visits to the list of recurrent expenses (as a business owner, I have begun to think of medical bills as "just another person on the payroll!") and, as of the publication of this book, I have spent the 10 months seeing a multitude of doctors on a weekly basis. I have experienced a long list of fluctuating symptoms and I have had exorbitant amounts of bloodwork, tests, and scans done. I have felt sick, swollen, empty, foggy, and fatigued. Some days, I feel nothing like myself and could barely remember what feeling "normal" feels like. On my work days, I would try to think straight, but my thoughts were being diverted by many walls. It was exhausting and scary. The worst part is that it feels like a lifetime ago when I last looked and felt like myself. In so many ways, I was living in the past. There was my life pre-miscarriage and my life post-miscarriage. Unfortunately, my health — and therefore my life — have yet to get back to normal since that defining moment, when my body said, "STOP."

In 2020, my life came to a screeching halt. I had been on the proverbial green light (chasing dreams, overachieving, never stopping to rest) for so many years that, as soon as I hit a red light with the pregnancy and miscarriage, my body finally had a break, and it was screaming at me to pay attention to it. Not only was I completely disconnected from my body all those years as I was just trying to survive, but I do believe that all my trauma was being hidden and stored so deep that I was functioning without asking my body if it needed rest. Down deep, I knew that if I stopped long enough to ask my body if it needed a break, the answer would be yes and a break would slow me down. In my mind, slowing down was a sign of weakness, and life was about running — to the tree stump, to the locked bathroom, up or down the 13 stairs, to the next challenge or achievement or deadline. When I did finally slow down, I realized I had been making myself sick — for as long as I could remember.

Connecting My Past to My Present

Before I adopted Cooper and before I met JP, I barely allowed myself to feel my own emotions. I had no problem feeling the emotions for *others* or having empathy. Likewise, it was always easy for me to *give* love, but it was impossible for me to receive love. I realized that receiving is the hard part — because in order to receive, I needed to feel.

 It was always easy for me to give love, but it was impossible for me to receive love. I realized that receiving is the hard part — because in order to receive, I needed to feel.

Before 2020, I barely allowed my body to tell me how it was feeling. I hardly felt fatigue or pain. Because the trauma I experienced as a child had taught me the skills I needed in order to survive, I became an expert at ignoring emotions, especially the ones that made me feel vulnerable and human. I was conditioned to push through stress, fear, pain, and fatigue.

Here I am now, decades later, making the connection between my past and my present. I see how my childhood made me independent, resilient, passionate, and driven. I see how my childhood prepared me for some of the most difficult challenges I would face as an adult. I feel like I can handle anything at 33, because of what I have already been taught. Thanks to the generosity of others, to my own fortitude, to a universe that is more generous than cruel, and sometimes to sheer, dumb luck, I was given the power to catapult change in a life that started out ill-fated and has become abundant with blessings. I was given the chance to turn 180 degrees — from past to present, from dark to light, from fear to fearless.

Every morning, when I make the turn out of the neighborhood to head to the office, I face the red light, taking 90 seconds to stare at the opposing attorneys' office, taking me right back to that lawsuit when I was 26, with the quickest reminder of what I have been through, what I have overcome, and the most important parts of the journey that I will never forget. Every weekend, when I run through the Forest Hill streets, I remember living in the cockroach-infested apartment by the train tracks, where I initially decided to turn left and run through this very neighborhood, dreaming of living here one day.

I sit here from my home office, typing on my computer, staring out the glass, seeing nothing but lush greenery and the old trees mimicking each other in the pond's reflection. I have found another safe spot — one shared with the trees and the water, in perfect silence.

EPILOGUE

November 19, 2020

"We are vacationers!"

At long last, I am taking a real break.

After finding an expired passport before our honeymoon last year, JP and I made a promise to each other that we would take one real, off-the-grid vacation every year, no matter what obstacles life tried to throw at us. In March of this year, we were faced with an obstacle larger than anything we could have ever imagined —the COVID-19 pandemic.

For those of us lucky enough to survive this year, COVID still stole health, well-being, time, celebrations, business, safety, security, families, holidays, and vacations from all of us. With a push from my therapist, JP and I were able to keep our promise to each other and plan the trip, but whether the trip could actually happen was out of our hands. Resorts were closing, as were international borders. We waited and we hoped.

As we entered the fall season, COVID had not only persevered through 2020 but it had escalated. Wave after wave of infections and deaths, and now the weather was turning cold again. No one but the truly daring or foolish was getting on an airplane just yet. But, in the middle of October, Costa Rica announced that they would open their borders to all visitors from the United States on November 1st. Our vacation —a trip to Costa Rica — was scheduled for November 13th. *Was it possible? Could we really go?* It was and we could. All our planned activities for this dream vacation were outdoors and we knew we would probably be among a small group traveling there. We gave it much consideration and thought we could keep ourselves and others safe. So we continued to keep our vacation promise and *vamos!* We entered the land of Pura Vida, intent on living the simple, pure life that Costa Ricans espouse.

I write to you here, from a van traveling on a bumpy mixture of paved and dirt roads, winding through the mountainous rainforest towns of Costa Rica. My cell phone has been off since we got here, and it remains inside our hotel room. My mind is clear, and I have more time to find true joy — like connecting with the people here. They are special. I have been so happy and I feel so free, after a few days of exploring and adventure, eating so much fresh pineapple and papaya, and finding my new favorite snack — plantain chips. I am scribbling on the back of my book manuscript in my red pen. It feels surreal to be here with JP, and to be writing to you — the readers of this book — while I breathe this fresh air and celebrate a present and future that eclipses the past that I survived.

Visually, Costa Rica offers an abundance of beauty and color. I feel inspired by the colorful fruit, woven tablecloths, beaded jewelry, rainbowed buildings, and flourishing flowers. There is so much water. There is so much green — my absolute favorite color.

Numerically, I am in awe. The magnitude of this bustling ecosystem is staggering. Everyone is pollinating — the 1,500 species of butterflies, the 850 species of birds, including more than 50 kinds of hummingbirds.

Audibly, our ears are dominated by the sounds, the music of the rainforest, which includes the humming, buzzing, howling, and hissing. There are so many sounds — silence doesn't live here, only the music.

Emotionally, I feel free.

Physically, I feel rested.

No matter where we go, the volcano is always present. I feel its strength. It has grounded me every time my mind wanders, when I shift my focus right back to it, staring at it up and down, feeling its height reaching through the clouds, toward the sun, and its base sitting happily amongst the most beautiful flora and fauna I have ever seen, in one of the most biodiverse places in the world. This is paradise, and we deserve this.

We are heading back to our hotel. Our tour guide, Hugo, has spent three days with us, showing us his country. We were his first tours since March, nearly eight months ago. Everything just opened back up here. Most Ticos (native Costa Ricans) work in tourism, so the shutdown due to the global pandemic was devastating to their country, and the emergency assistance from the government was reportedly not enough to keep most citizens afloat. Because we have everything to ourselves here, including the van, I have been asking Hugo a lot of questions, and I have learned so much. While we weren't sure about making the trip, I suddenly knew we were exactly where we were supposed to be when Hugo said, "You don't realize the hope you are giving us. Now that we have seen tourists, we have the optimism and hope that they will come back."

I tried to wipe my tears quickly. "They *will* come back, and they ARE coming back. Please, tell your family and friends that the tourists *are* coming back," I promised.

On our first day of adventure with Hugo, we hiked around the Arenal Volcano, which was in an eruptive cycle from 1968 until late 2010 and has been in a resting phase for the past decade. I took note: even volcanos can take a much-needed rest.

On our way up the volcano, we saw two moving lines, one forward and one backward, of leafcutter ants traveling the distance of a mile — according to Hugo, a feat they perform only by scent because they are blind. We touched "touch-me-not" plants that shriveled up instantly when you touched them. And we marveled at the discovery that Hugo can replicate almost any animal sound. He howled for the howler monkeys and they answered. He showed us how connected the Ticos are with nature — they don't fear it, but they appreciate it. He continued to grab large spiders and allow them to climb up his arm until he placed them back in their webs.

There was sunlight pouring through, as the forest kept its openness to the view of the volcano.

Hugo shared, "There are no seasons here, only dry and wet, so the trees don't have rings, because they are constantly growing."

I could not help but catch the metaphor.

Hugo shared, "There are no seasons here, only dry and wet, so the trees don't have rings, because they are constantly growing."

I could not help but catch the metaphor.

We continued our hike up to a plateau, which overlooks the Lago Arenal (lake) on the western side of the volcano. We stood on volcanic rock and took some photos as the sun was setting over the lake. As we headed down from that scenic point, we entered a series of natural pathways through the rainforest that were so heavily covered that, at dusk, it seemed much later. Our surroundings were lush leaves, hanging and twisted vines, and large Ficus trees that looked like animal houses. The more we walked, the deeper in the rainforest we were.

"Here in Costa Rica, we believe that for every two hours in the rainforest, your cells in your lungs regenerate for two weeks. The rainforest cleans and heals your lungs."

His words resonated deeply, as I kept picturing my lungs being cleaned out with the swirling pattern of clean air and new green cells. *How many hours would I need to spend in the rainforest to clean out my lungs from my first 18 years?*

As we continued to make our way back down the volcano, we were about to leave the rainforest trail when Hugo told us to stop. "Take a few minutes to meditate and connect with the nature surrounding us," he implored. And so we did.

Hugo went down the trail. JP and I stayed and slowly separated ourselves. We stared at the flora and fauna that surrounded us. I faced the volcano, keeping my back toward JP as he faced the small body of water in front of him. I closed my eyes, held out my hands, and kept my palms facing up. I was soaking it all in, and I could not stop crying.

During our last rainforest excursion, we opted for something a little more daring. I had my fanny bag packed with hand sanitizer, a mask, Chapstick, and a split of Costa Rican colóns and U.S. dollars. It was November in Costa Rica, which is at the end of its wet season, so it was raining, and the

cloud of fog was just
a floating layer hanging
well above the canopy.
I had my helmet on
and a safety belt that
was connected by two
carabiners to a small set
of metal handlebars. My
hands grabbed tightly
as I traversed via zipline
for one mile, 650 feet

Vacation hike at Arenal Volcano,
Costa Rica, November 2020

above the rainforest canopy, where I could not see ahead of me, beside me,
or under me. I was living in the moment — moment after moment as the
visuals and sounds and aromas sped by. On a zipline, there is no going back,
and it is hard to look back when you are propelling forward at such a high
speed. I kept looking forward, soaking it all in.

I was completely engulfed for the opaque blanket of fog. I can't help but
think that this was just like life — I could never see what was ahead. Behind
me, it was just a cloud, but I had to trust that I would come out on the other
side of the fog, for a safe landing, and that I was in control. Everything
would be OK.

**I had to trust that I would come out on the other
side of the fog, for a safe landing, and that
I was in control. Everything would be OK.**

Hugo doesn't know that I wrote down the things he said. He also
doesn't know that he is in the epilogue of my book (or even that I wrote
a book), but I plan to surprise *mi amigo nuevo.*

Being in Costa Rica held a certain significance for me. It was not just
a vacation. The rainforest had everything I needed to heal, and it
came at a perfect time, after finishing this book, and battling a year of
less-than-perfect health.

Costa Rica brought me right back to my hill in the woods, surrounded by
trees, overlooking the creek and hearing nothing but its rushing water,

moving stronger after it rained, cascading over each and every rock that stood in its way. With no distractions, life was so simple and humble here, as I felt the connection to who I am at my core, with the connection to nature, the sounds of safety, and the clean air.

I used to feel like my adult life was poisoned by my childhood life, which included the dark and painful feelings of guilt, shame, and hate. After peeling back so many layers of my experiences and my internal stories — connecting the dots and finding the meaning behind each layer — I found purpose in my past, which included a new belief that there was value in sharing my story. By sharing my story verbally through public speaking, I felt the grime shedding off, and I felt the stains coming out. I feel pure for the first time. Pura vida, as the Ticos taught me.

In reading this book, I know I have taken you to some dark places and some painful stories. But as you prepare to set the book down and close its pages for the last time, I want you to know that I am OK now. I am happy. I am fulfilled on all levels and I am surrounded by incredible people, like my husband, our precious dogs, and my dear friends.

I always wanted a real family. And a safe, loving home. Today, I have both. I have many families now — my work family, my gym family, my networking family, my Toastmasters family, and my dance family (with my own recitals behind me, now I teach!). I have been adopted many times, so I have parents, grandparents, siblings, nieces, and nephews.

Home.

I get to work with the best people every day. I get to create homes for my clients, the dream I have had since watching *Trading Spaces* when I was 13. My clients talk and I see, as my brain paints pictures that sometimes foreshadows their story. I see their home in my head, months before they see it in real life. That is my gift, and I think it's because I spent so many years dreaming up one for me — more than just a house, but a home. Working from the penciled sketches on vellum through to the final "pillow chop" is what feeds my soul to work as hard as I do. (Oh, and I do two hits on center for the best pillow chop!)

I am living a completely different life than I was even two years ago. I can receive love now, which means I actually FEEL ... and my emotions are very active these days!

It has been a long, difficult, and painful journey to get here, but having a story is much better than not having a story. I have put in the work. I have surrounded myself with the right people and after many mistakes and failures, I finally got it right. I am taking care of myself now. I am ready to start our family and I am ready to be the best mom — the one I never had.

You know what is so great about all of this? My past made me who I am, and it gave me everything I have today. My past paid for my future. My past fueled my passions and set me up for a life *full* of passion. I am done running. I am done hiding. I have turned — not just left or right, but 180 degrees. And the view from here is spectacular.

My past made me who I am, and it gave me everything I have today. My past paid for my future.

ACKNOWLEDGMENTS

Thank you to those who embraced me, loved me, and believed in me, becoming part of the family I was lucky enough to create. Thank you to my sisters, Lauren, Kellie, and Meleah, for giving me the opportunity to be Auntie Danielle to my beautiful nephews Everett and Casler, and nieces Katie and Raiden.

Thank you to Lucinda and Eugene for believing in a 25-year-old Danielle to pay you back a large business loan while I was able to follow my dreams and become an entrepreneur — something that never seemed possible.

Thank you to Paul Bail for trusting in me and allowing my college education dreams to come true, with you as my student loan co-signer.

Thank you to my PCDG team for being loyal, hardworking, and showing the world about integrity.

Thank you to my husband, JP, for challenging me and putting up with the worst in me to see the best in me.

Thank you to Wilmington Toastmasters for giving me a safe space and supporting me from the first day I began publicly sharing my story, and to Rob Campbell for telling me that I was ready to tell my story to the world and putting me in touch with a women-run publishing company.

You have all changed the course of my life and shown me what a family really is.

Keep in Touch!

Can you relate to my story?

 Please reach out if you feel inclined. I need stories to relate to as well, so let's story swap! You're not alone; I'm not alone; we're in this beautiful journey together.

Public speaking is my jam!

 Please reach out if you know of any opportunities where you feel my story would benefit an audience. It would be my honor.

Find me here!

 DanielleSaintardValiente.com

Interested in how I give back to the amazing and brave children?

I write stories for them, which you can find here:

 SmunchkinLearns.com

ABOUT THE AUTHOR

Danielle Saintard Valiente is an interior designer, entrepreneur, and author who resides in Wilmington, North Carolina, with her husband Jean-Pierre and their dogs Cruz and Clarke Kent.

Danielle was born and raised in Leominster, Massachusetts, where she left for college without looking back, receiving her Bachelor of Science in Interior Design from Endicott College in 2010. The day of graduation, Danielle had her car packed to move down to Wilmington, sight unseen.

Since living in North Carolina, Danielle has opened an interior design firm, Port City Design Group, started several product lines, and written a children's book series entitled *Smunchkin Learns*. She has immersed herself in her local community while enjoying extracurricular activities, which include weightlifting, being a hip-hop dance teacher, and serving on the boards of her local Toastmasters club and the Cape Fear Literacy Council. Danielle also holds an annual fundraiser for The Carousel Center, a local nonprofit that serves child survivors of sexual and domestic abuse.

Danielle looks forward to continuing her personal journey through reading, writing, and speaking while traveling, connecting, and inspiring children, students, and aspiring entrepreneurs around the world.

Made in the USA
Columbia, SC
08 December 2021